DISCARD

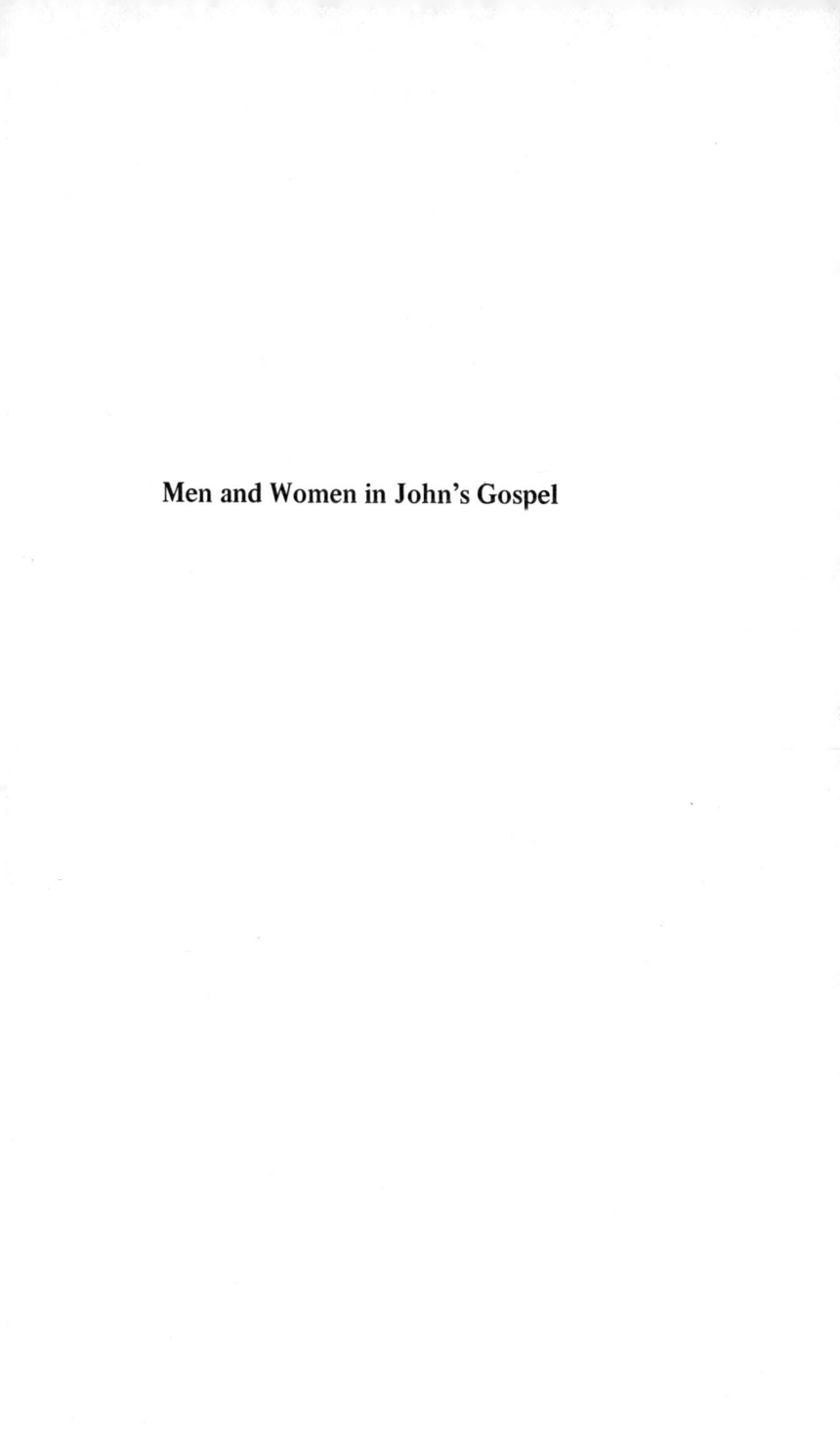

Men and Women in John's Gospel

Men & Women
in JOHN'S GOSPEL

Jerry M. Self

BROADMAN PRESS • Nashville, Tennessee

© Copyright 1974 • Broadman Press
All rights reserved
ISBN: 0-8054-8123-0
4281-23

Library of Congress Catalog Card Number: 74-79487
Dewey Decimal Classification: 225.92
Printed in the United States of America

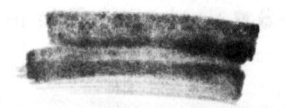

To
the people of
Austin Heights Baptist Church

Acknowledgments

Quotations in this book are from the following sources and are used by permission as indicated.

Scripture quotations, unless otherwise indicated, are from the *Today's English Version* of the New Testament. Copyright © American Bible Society 1966, 197.

Pages 37-38
>   Chester Todd, "The Christology of Albert Schweitzer" (Unpublished paper, Southwestern Baptist Theological Seminary).

Pages 59-61
>   William Glasser, *Reality Therapy* (New York: Harper & Row, Publishers, 1965), pp. 9, 92.

Page 61
>   Rabbi Abraham Heschel, "The Abiding Challenge of Religion," *The Center Magazine*, March/April, 1973, p. 47.

Pages 70, 118
>   From *The Gospel of John*, Volume 2, translated and interpreted by William Barclay. Published in the U.S.A. by The Westminster Press, 1958.

Contents

1. The Subordinate 17
2. Discipling 23
3. He Understands Me 29
4. The Civilized Christian 35
5. Significant Living 43
6. No Cheap Tricks 51
7. The Man or the System? 57
8. The Squareroot of Blindness 63
9. The Realist and the Mystic 67
10. A Family Affair 75
11. What Are You Made Of? 81
12. Rude Arrogance 89
13. What Is Truth? 95
14. Beyond Skepticism 101
15. Searching for Death; Finding Life 109
16. The Gift of Clear Thought 115
17. Discipling Love 121

Introduction

I have been impressed with the character development in the book of John. Aristotle contends that of the six parts which make up a tragedy, "plot" is of first importance and "characters" is second. It would appear that the Synoptic Gospels outline the plot of the gospel and name its chief character while the Fourth Gospel supplies the other characters.

In comparison with the Synoptics, John has fewer total individuals—only 38 in John contrasting with 71 in Matthew, 69 in Mark, and 110 in Luke—but he has developed more "live" personalities.

The Fourth Gospel shows more facets to the characters which are prominent in all four Gospels and also develops people who are only mentioned in the other Gospels. All told, John lists only seven disciples by name: Simon Peter, Andrew, Philip, Thomas, Nathanael, and the two Judases—one Iscariot and the other not. But four disciples, Andrew, Philip, Thomas, and Nathanael, who are no more than names in the Synoptics—in fact "Nathanael" is not even a name in the other three Gospels—gain personality in the Gospel of John.

There are four major personalities appearing in the Fourth Gospel which are not found in the other Gospels: Nicodemus, the Samaritan woman, the man born blind, and Lazarus. Only the Fourth Gospel names Peter as the disciple who strikes and Malchus as the high priest's slave who is struck during the arrest scene in the garden. Yet, surprisingly, in the Gospel which shows the most character development, the author never uses the name "Mary" in describing the mother of Jesus. This seems a bit odd in view of the fact that two stories are told about her not found elsewhere: the wedding feast miracle at Cana and the adoption ceremony at the cross. Some commentators think that the author does not name anyone who happens to be a relative of his. This theory makes the apostle John a cousin of Jesus and therefore requires that Mary's name not be mentioned. Although this hypothesis may be no more than the product of a healthy imagination, the suggestion is provocative and illustrates the many theories, speculations, and legends which have grown up about this rich and often mysterious Gospel.

I mention these things to prick your curiosity about biblical studies. There is no end to the variety of paths which might be pursued in a study of the Gospel of John, but here are some brief observations from my own study.

The Fourth Gospel deals with fewer personalities than the Synoptics, thus allowing for fuller development of the people who are included. Even though Luke gives the largest number of names, it is characteristically an anonymous Gospel. One quarter of those names serve only as reference points to the story and are not participants. Many of the people in Luke's story are simply "a man who . . ." or "a certain woman." There are a few people without names in John's Gospel but they are by no means anonymous. Even without a name for the Samaritan woman, we feel that we know her quite well.

By showing us fewer but more developed personalities, the Fourth Gospel lends a different quality to the description of Jesus. In the Synoptics Jesus is the only personality developed. One sees him moving quickly, teaching and healing, dying and rising. Other personalities are simply a blurred background.

John slows the story to fewer figures and events. The result is that we see a few people very well and, in them, ourselves reflected quite clearly. We also catch some richer hues in the portrait of the Master. John adds to our picture of the Lord highlights, shadings, richness.

The characters he presents provide vivid contrast to one another as well as to Jesus. One of the earlier and more marked contrasts is found in the movement from chapter 3 to 4, from Nicodemus to the Samaritan woman. He is not only a man, but a distinguished rabbi; she is not only a woman—cause for being second-class in her world—but a nameless tramp. The scenes intensify the contrast: Jerusalem as opposed to the proximity of Gerizim, the Samaritan holy place. But in either case the characters gain an insight into the spiritual dimensions of life from the skilled Teacher who speaks everyone's language.

Watch for other contrasts in the Fourth Gospel: the personal approach of Jesus to the lame and the blind men as opposed to an uncaring crowd, the perception of the blind man which exceeds the vision of others, the busyness of Martha and the contemplation of Mary. The Gospel story opens with the disciples of John graduating to become followers of Jesus. The Baptist is compared with the Savior. Later, Caiaphas and Pilate are given less favorable comparisons as the priest and the governor pass judgment on the Lord. At numerous points along the way a disciple will step apart from the group either in contrast with them, as seen in the case of Thomas, or as representative, as seen in the stories of Philip, Andrew, and Peter.

The following are studies of different encounters Jesus had with the people of the Fourth Gospel. In some the focus is on the Master while in others it falls on his companion of the moment. May they help you to understand him, and them, and yourself a bit better.

Men and Women in John's Gospel

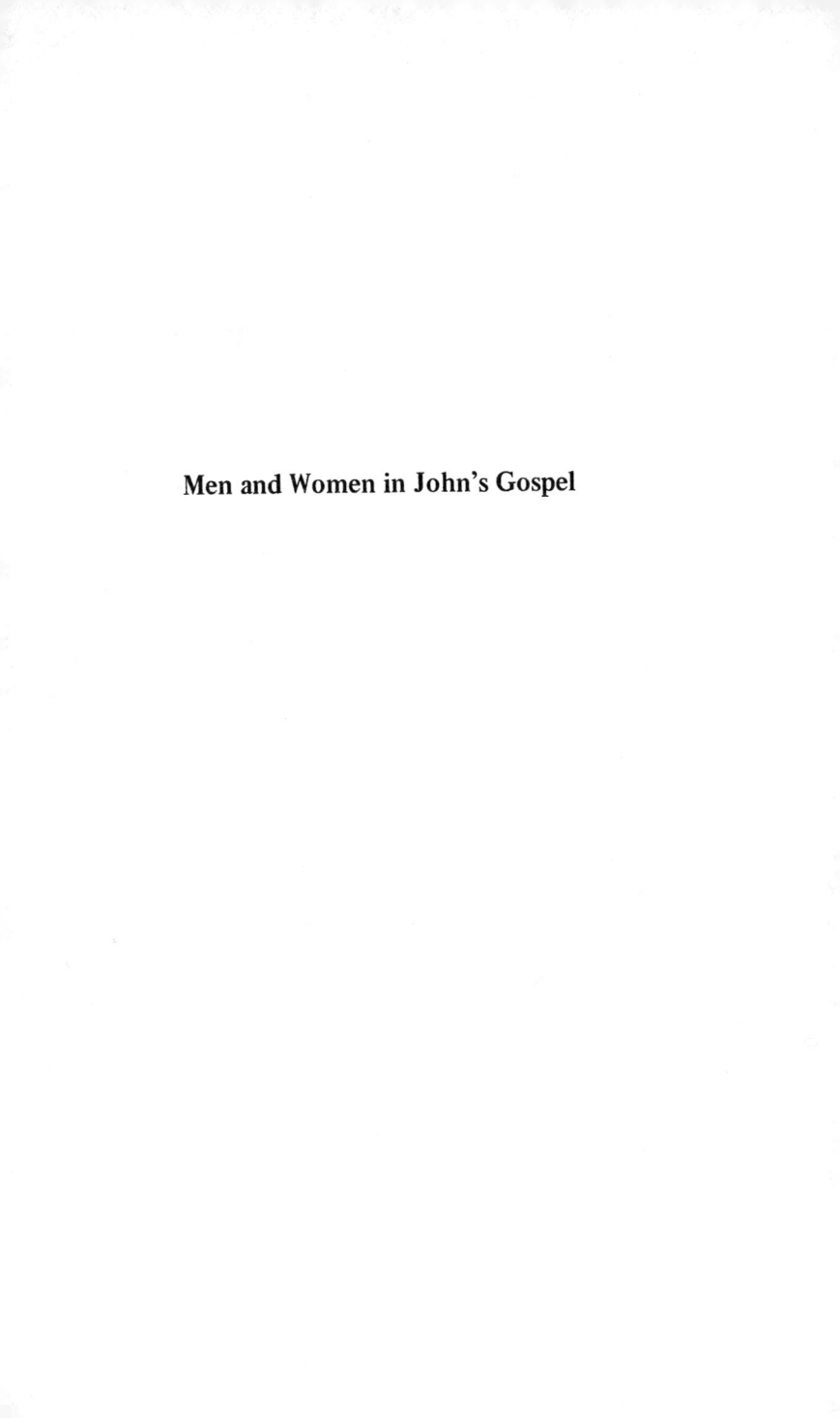

The Subordinate

He must become more important, while I become less important.   John 3:30

Some men find many causes and many campaigns in life. Their days are filled with variety and versatility. Others fight for only one cause. From beginning to end their lives know only one theme. God makes use of both of these types. Michelangelo was a painter, sculptor, architect, inventor. His life shone with many colors. On the other hand, John the Baptist had but one task in life. The entirety of his existence was consumed in the capacity of being the forerunner of the Christ. The whole of his life can be described in his well-known statement: "He must increase; I must decrease!" or as *Today's English Version* has it, "He must become more important, while I become less important."

Many of us like to think of ourselves as Michelangelo types: the Renaissance man, he who knows the important things about every subject. The truth is that we are more inclined the other way. Ours is a society of specialists. We number among us, however, too few specialists in excellence. My crowd is filled with those who are ignorant in general and mediocre in particular. John the Baptist could serve as an appropriate model for the specialist.

John the Baptist performs a significant role in the Fourth Gospel and he does it well. I believe this to be true although there is some question about John's place in the Fourth Gospel. The major characters in the Gospel of John show more development than they are given in the Synoptics except for John the Baptist. Perhaps this is because the author is attempting to counteract a sect that was building up around the veneration of John the Baptist as the Messiah. The book of Acts and the writings of Justin Martyr tell of persons who knew only the baptism of John the Baptist. By the third century or later there appears to have been a sect devoted to the Baptist. Thus it could be that John the Baptist is minimized in the Fourth Gospel in an effort to play down a potential rival messiah.

Though this theory is quite plausible, the fact remains that John the Baptist plays a significant role in this gospel. He has a vital witness concerning Jesus. John is mentioned in four places and each of these passages is shorter than the preceding ones. Is this a stylistic way of emphasizing John's own testimony that Jesus must become more important while he became less important?

Perhaps the picture of John the Baptist given in the Fourth Gospel is not a less-developed personality but a more intensified one. Usually most of us make a distinction between who we are and what we do; but John's essence was captured in his function. Who he was and what he did were synonymous. He is presented as a first century "Johnny One-Note." By showing us this insight into the baptizer, the Fourth Gospel may be taking us to the heart of the personality of this man.

I have discovered three characteristics of John the Baptist.

John the Baptist had a vivid sense of being commissioned.
He was called and he knew it. He had a stronge sense that he had been authorized by God to do what he was doing. In John 1:6 he is described as "a man sent by God." In John 1:33 he speaks of "one who sent me" and in John 3:28 the Baptist

The Subordinate

tells his disciples that he has been "sent ahead of" the Messiah.

This strong sense of authority was a stabilizing factor for John during stress. He was grilled about his authority for his actions but it did not upset his sense of calling. The questioning by the religious authorities was quite proper because John had been teaching, which was the function of an ordained rabbi, and he had been performing the Jewish ritual of immerion. Any charlatan who had any doubts about the propriety of his actions would have gone weak-in-the-knees before such duly constituted authority. But not John the Baptist. He felt secure in his actions.

And that brings up another point. *John the Baptist had a clear understanding of his task.* He knew exactly what it was he had to do. His role as the forerunner to the Messiah is parallel to that of one who preceded a king and straightened the roads so that they would be suitable for the king. The prophecy that a messenger would be sent ahead of the Messiah was almost a threat. The messenger was coming to institute a general housecleaning. But there is also an overtone of hope. Isaiah spoke of the preparation of a way through the desert for the people to return from captivity to their homes. John comes as the forerunner to prepare a way for God to visit his people in the form of the Messiah.

As forerunner to the Messiah his task is simply to witness to the Christ. He testifies that the coming one is the Lamb of God, that he has experienced life before us, that his life is activated by the Spirit of God, and he is a specially chosen person.

John is quite aware of the distinctions between his task and that of the Messiah. "I baptize you with water to show that you have repented," he announces to his hearers, "but the one who will come after me will baptize you with the Holy Spirit." What a perceptive insight is this. "All I can do is engage in symbolic ritual. He will bring the significance to your lives." This theme characterizes the appearance of John in this gospel.

"I am the reflector. He is the Light."

"I am the voice. He is the Word."

"I am the custodian of the symbol. He is the Possessor of Meaning."

It must seem obvious from what has been said so far that *John the Baptist recognized his subordinate status.* Such a recognition helps at all levels.

For one thing, John knew who he was not and what he was not to do. He disclaims any role or identification which will bring attention to himself. Israel had waited four hundred years since the last prophet had spoken. Suddenly a new voice is heard and he is obviously a voice from God. Josephus indicates that the Jewish people were quite excited over John the Baptist. In fact, they were so taken with John's appearance that a committee comes to him with the question, "Are you the Messiah?" What an opportunity to put himself in high office.

But his answer is a simple, "I am not the Christ!"

"Are you Elijah, then?"

"No, I am not!"

"Well," they wanted to know, "Just who do you think you are?"

The humility of his answer is embarrassing to those of us who are so eager to present our credentials to a status-conscious world.

"This is what I am: 'The voice of one who shouts in the desert: Make a straight path for the Lord to travel!'"

John plainly feels that he is not worthy of the office of slave to the Messiah. Compare his reverence of the Christ to a remark by a third-century rabbi. "Every service which a slave performs for his master a pupil will do for his teacher, except loosing his shoe," taught the rabbi. But John said, "He comes after me, but I am not good enough even to untie his sandals."

Later in his ministry, when his disciples will become jealous because Jesus is gaining more recruits than John, he will say,

The Subordinate

"He is the bridegroom. I am just a friend at the wedding and I am glad to hear the bridegroom's voice." The Gospel spotlight lingers on John only long enough for him to suggest to some of his disciples it would be better for them to take up with Jesus than to stay with him.

At the time, the people did not quite know what to do with such honesty and humility but later they came to appreciate it. The Fourth Gospel records in chapter 10 that many people acknowledged: "John did no mighty works . . . but everything he said about this man was true. And many people believed in him." The integrity of John's witness influenced these listeners toward Jesus the Christ.

How can I be as clearheaded about life as John the Baptist? Perhaps our hyperactive twentieth-century setting is so far from John's life that it is impossible to act and speak with the authoritative precision that marked his life. Or perhaps we can be equally clearheaded. Let me ask you to try on three thoughts and see how they fit.

Consider your position in respect to God. John's sense of subordination indicates a sound understanding of what this world is all about. Humanity is neither self-sufficient nor an end in itself. When we discover our subordination to God, we have taken a first step toward clearheadedness.

Consider your understanding of Jesus Christ. John's example was to be focused on Jesus Christ. He found definition for personality and vocation in Jesus Christ. There may be some clues for you in the realization that Jesus was a finely developed human personality. Focusing on him will help clarify life.

Consider yourself–both essence and function, who are you and what can you do–*and decide where you fit into the scope of God's world.* One commentator has observed the remarkable witness of John that he was pleased to rejoice with the Messiah like a friend at a wedding. This is a rare talent. We are more inclined to weep with those in sorrow than to rejoice with those who are happy. To prove this think of the different words that speak of sharing another's pain—sympathy, compassion and the like—and then try to find a comparable term that means sharing another's happiness. (Rejoice indicates joy but not sharing.) This rare talent was one gift which John had to contribute. If you will determine your gifts while conscious of your relation to God and your understanding of Jesus Christ, you just might end up with a strong sense of calling about your life.

To do all this considering requires some reflective time. Perhaps the desert experience of John the Baptist is what kept him from being a repugnant know-it-all. He has the proper blend of humility and authority that makes his message convincing.

There are some optical illusions that are hard to inspect because they make your eyes move in a direction away from the center of the picture. John is like that. As we attempt to look at him we cannot because we follow his outstretched arm and pointing finger and hear his words: "Here is the Lamb of God who takes away the sin of the world."

Our view of Jesus grows as John passes from sight.

Discipling

For a long time I have been with you all; yet you do not know . . . ? John 14:9

Both learning and teaching require more of us than we are usually willing to admit. James Boswell was enamored enough with Samuel Johnson that he wrote a biography of the remarkable man; however, Boswell conceded that Johnson had gained his knowledge "by fits and starts, by violent irruptions into the regions of knowledge; and it could not be expected that his impatience would be subdued, and his impetuosity restrained, so as to fit him for a quiet guide to novices." Whatever there was for Boswell to commend about Johnson, he could not, in honesty, consider Johnson an able teacher.

Philip and Andrew afford us an opportunity to consider the learning-teaching relationship of Jesus and his disciples. At the heart of the term "disciple" is the connotation of teaching-learning. These two disciples come to life in the Fourth Gospel where they often stand as representative of the twelve. They are seen together coming to Jesus and bringing others, puzzling over the hungry hoard around Jesus, and introducing some Greeks to the Master. Finally Philip is paired with Thomas in asking questions in a closing teaching moment.

The gradual growth of the disciples throughout the Gospel

reminds us that *learning is a life-long process.* In the first chapter of the book you read of John the Baptist pointing his disciples toward Jesus. As these men become acquainted with the new teacher, there are recurring expressions which become thematic. A sequence is repeated where one goes to Jesus and is invited to "come and follow." This is answered, as John's Gospel puts it, by the disciple doing just that, following. "Following Jesus" becomes symbolic of growth as a disciple.

As a first step in growth, these disciples immediately respond to the new teacher with a desire to share their new relationship. Andrew goes to find his brother Simon. Philip finds Nathanael. When Nathanael puts up some sort of challenge to what Philip is advertising, Philip exercises one of the primary techniques of learning. In a life situation he mimics his teacher. The disciples had questioned Jesus and had received his invitation to Nathanael, "Come and see." Mimicry and personal experience—basic tools of education—will serve to help the disciples grow as they follow the Master Teacher.

The father of Laurence Sterne's character Tristram Shandy speaks of his concern that his son have a suitable tutor. He looked upon this person "as the mirror in which [the son] is to view himself from morning to night, and by which he is to adjust his looks, his carriage, and perhaps the inmost sentiments of his heart." For that reason this father wanted a teacher "polished at all points, fit for my child to look into." If the parents of Philip and Andrew had a similar desire for their sons (surely they did), could they have chosen a better instructor than the young Galilean carpenter?

How skillful was Jesus as teacher? On one occasion a large crowd surrounded him to learn from him. Does popularity answer the question of value? Probably not. He didn't keep the crowds long. If the Messiah were an office which came before the voters every four years as does the Presidency, Jesus would not have been reelected. But back to that crowd. In the morning Jesus mentioned to Philip that such a large group

Discipling

would need to be fed and did he have any suggestions. Apparently, as the various accounts of this story are compared, there was a sufficient interval of time between this proposal of the problem and the actual time when food was required to allow the disciples to put their heads together. Philip had immediately seen that a large amount of money would only provide a bare minimum of bread for the mob. But, except for that bookkeeper's evaluation of the predicament, he has no more to offer. Andrew has found a young man with a lunch but he concludes that it doesn't amount to anything in the face of such a large crowd. In their pessimism, these two are representative of the twelve. No one else does any better.

Does it seem just a little strange that some of the disciples, certainly Philip and Andrew, had attended the wedding celebration at Cana but had no idea as to how the crowd might be fed? There are various levels of lessons here. The disciples are slow to recognize the providing power of their leader-teacher. After long years of study, the author of this Gospel has gained the insight to put together rather closely two miracles: the provision of wine at Cana and the provision of bread in chapter 6. In these miracles of provision shines the deeper lesson of the ultimate provision resident in the blood and body of the Redeemer. But Philip and Andrew have not reached that level of understanding yet.

How many other opportunities are there for teaching? How many different methods employed by the great Rabbi? What growth is there and how painful or slow? The evangelist warns us away from such speculation by saying that the life of Jesus cannot be condensed to any one book. Indeed, all the books in this world could not begin to tell his story. But still, we wonder.

Late in his ministry, or, if you prefer, later in their following, some Gentiles seek out a disciple who has a Gentile name and they ask Philip to present them to his teacher. But Philip is aware that Jesus has said some peculiar things about when he would be ready to teach Gentiles and he was not sure the time was right. So Philip consults with his trusty companion Andrew and together they approach Jesus with some strange faces in tow.

Speaking of strange faces, what an unusual look came over the Master's face! And what an odd exclamation! Jesus sees the approach of Gentiles and cries out something about the arrival of "his hour." It is as though some sacred moment is impending. What is there lurking in the shadows which arouses Jesus through the appearance of these Greeks?

We are coming toward the close of the course, and the material weighs heavy on minds not sufficiently stout for the task. There are object lessons and lectures which seem to point toward a great final exam, some austere oral test in which these meagre "C" students will be challenged to come up to the standards of an imposing graduate committee. Philip has gotten lost in an obscure reference to footnotes or number of absences allowed and he struggles to cut to the heart of the curriculum. "Just show us the Father," he interrupts, "and I believe I can catch up with the class." What a fumbling request! But what a revealing response! "That is what I have been doing all semester, Philip. I am showing you the Father." Perhaps Philip caught on . . . or perhaps he did not.

You see, Philip and Andrew represent the second rank of disciples. They are sometimes screened out by such notables as Peter or John who are acclaimed for their gospel work or by Judas who is infamous for his betrayal. These back row disciples never have the starring role but they still perform a service. They are slow but willing learners. Philip does not appear quick-witted. He is serious enough and concerned, but he seems gifted only at missing the point. Maybe he never got it all together, but he still had his contribution to make.

Andrew was a trusted counselor. He is attractive because he found it natural to introduce people to Jesus. Philip sometimes misses the point, but he is a dependable follower and has a devout faith. They may not ever have mastered all that could have been learned from Jesus, but does that invalidate their place in his kingdom's work?

By observing these disciples you may be reminded of the lifelong process of learning. If so, it is helpful to realize the quality of our guide on the journey. To be sure, the ability to learn is, in no small way, dependent on the skill of the one teaching. Aristotle was the teacher of Alexander the Great. Alexander expressed a love for Aristotle equal to that he felt for his father because the one had given him life and the other had taught him to live well.

Jesus is a patient teacher. When first the disciples approached him, Jesus asked them what they wanted. He challenged them by his greeting to consider the object of their search. As they company together Jesus shows his confidence in himself as teacher and in them as learners by presenting a problem and leaving them with it to experience personally the frustration of learning in the act of living. After the Greeks intrude into his ministry, Jesus allows his followers to overhear his prayed concern at that critical moment. Surely that must have been an instructive experience, to have seen and heard the intensity of Jesus as he turned heavenward upon the awareness that he was encountering the threshhold of the climax of his ministry. Later he jars Philip some, though not harshly, when he is startled by Philip's obtuseness. Perhaps Philip had partially learned his lessons with the result that he expected an Exodus theophany: a burning bush, a pillar of fire, or a hovering cloud. Certainly he showed considerable faith even though he is only on the periphery of the lesson.

Gossip reflects on a story from the life of Confucius. Though a gentle teacher, he was once irritated by a pupil's dullness. The great philosopher complained that he could not continually repeat his lessons. If he successfully exposed one corner of a subject, then the pupil was expected to find the other three for himself. Slowness of learning is an excruciating challenge to the teacher. To be successful one must have the skill of patience.

Rousseau counted his father as a great teacher, a better teacher, in fact, than he was a student. But he concluded that "whatever propensity one may have to vice, it is not easy for an education, with which love has been mingled, to be entirely thrown away." Perhaps that is the secret to patient teaching. Philip, Andrew, and the others would have felt it daily. No matter how well or how poorly they mastered the lessons of life which Jesus set before them, they would know that their Master Teacher loved them.

He Understands Me!

How do you know me? John 1:48

Philip has discovered the Messiah and he wishes to share this news with his friend. But he disappoints Nathanael when he uses lofty titles to describe a carpenter from Nazareth. It is though he had proclaimed: "The next president of the United States, I give you a cabinetmaker from Nat. Would you believe an electrician from Wetumke? A plumber from Bug Tussle?" It is ludicrous nonsense. It is vaudeville. But the surprise is that Nathanael, though skeptical, is still open-minded enough to follow Philip to see what the excitement is.

Here is another passage from the Fourth Gospel with a great number of mysteries in it. Who was Nathanael? When he comes to Jesus, he is struck by the revelation that Jesus knows about Nathanael's experience under the fig tree; but we don't know about it. What happened under that fig tree? What was so special about Jesus knowing of it? In other words, why was Nathanael so stirred by Jesus' remark? There have been many attempts to explain all of this, and they are all imaginative speculations. The truth is that we can never know what is being shared between Jesus and Nathanael. Nevertheless the important thing for us is to capture the awareness that a spark jumped between them. The content of that event is known only to Nathanael and Jesus. But we can know the *meaning* of the event.

The meaning of that meeting has to do with communication. John's great message in this book is that the Word has come into the world. Jesus is God's communication with his people. As the communication, the Word of God, Jesus fulfills two functions of personal relationship.

He is performing the first responsibility of communicator when *Jesus hears.* This is good news. It is old news. It is as old as Genesis 21 where you can read the story of Hagar being expelled into the desert by jealous Sarah. Hagar abandoned her son under a bush because she could not stand to hear his dying moans. But out in that desert she received the message that God could hear the child even if she had gotten out of hearing range, and the child lived.

When we speak of Jesus being the Word of God, we seldom consider the fact that being a communicator involves hearing, but it does. Nathanael was heard by Jesus at a heart level. The spirit of Nathanael was heard by Jesus. This is what stirred him so, the realization that Jesus had heard the inner man. I remember hearing my pastor quote the psalmist's "deep answering unto deep" and wondering what that could possibly mean. Nathanael knew. It burst into his life suddenly as he encountered a man who responded to the deep recesses of his soul.

There is an interesting contrast in what these two men have to say to one another. Nathanael is so struck by Jesus that he calls him the Son of God. Jesus is so taken with Nathanael that he announces his own choice of titles and calls himself the Son of man.

Nathanael senses that he is heard. Such a needed, overwhelming experience causes him to exclaim that this man before him is a divine visitor, a unique representative of God. His insight is a declaration to us that one side of understanding

He Understands Me!

God's communication to us is to realize that Jesus does come from God. He is God's representative to be God's ears.

Jesus is pleased with the receptivity of this man who could overcome prejudice. It was not easy for Nathanael to come to Jesus. Galilee had produced only hotheaded false messiahs, as Nathanael would know. His hometown was close enough to Nazareth in the heart of Galilee to insure that Nathanael knew too well the lack of promise which was there. But he was willing to give Jesus a try. Nathanael has thus shown an unusual ability to hear Jesus and therefore the Master opens up to Nathanael more quickly than to other disciples seen in this Gospel.

The title which Jesus chose for himself, the Son of man, was derived from the Old Testament, primarily from the book of Daniel. It is part of the recurrent Old Testament messianic theme and has varied significance. In contrast to Nathanael's exclamation that Jesus is the Son of God, it can mean that another side of God's communication with man is the fact that Jesus has come to his people. He is thoroughly identified with humanity. It is not enough that we know God's representative hears. We want also to know that he hears us.

Jesus is one of us. How could it be otherwise if he intends to hear us? He intends to hear us? How could it be otherwise if he intends to speak to us?

Perhaps there is an important clue here about communication. Anybody who has said anything about conversation has at some point made a crack about all those people who only let other people talk in order to give themselves time to think of something else to say. It's true. Most of us do not listen. And for some reason, the less people listen, the more people talk. But the amazing thing is that once you sense that you have been heard, some of the pressure to talk is relieved and you can hear the other person. It is because Nathanael knew that Jesus had heard not only the pattern of his words but the rhythm of his heart that Nathanael was open and free to hear what Jesus had to say to him.

I have known this experience. I took a pressure cooker full of built-up emotion tightly sealed within me into a group of ministers in North Carolina. In that gathering of caring brothers the cork blew and some of the pressure was let off. I was heard. And somehow being heard cleaned out my own ears. I suddenly found that I was free and open to hear what they had to say to me.

Contradictory as it may sound, the good news is that the Word came hearing. But the completion of the story is to say the obvious. John calls Jesus the Word because *Jesus tells.* Another contrast in the conversation between Nathanael and Jesus helps us here. Because Nathanael was able to be openminded about coming to Jesus, Jesus hailed him as a genuine Israelite who had no guile. Nathanael responded that Jesus is the genuine king of the true Israel. Nathanael understood quickly what Pilate could never fathom even though Jesus would tell him plainly that he was a different kind of king. Jesus applauded Nathanael's openness and responsiveness and predicted further revelations of God's activities for those who were as receptive as Nathanael.

Jesus tells us two things, among many others, which we desperately want to hear. He accepts Nathanael's announcement that he is a true king to tell us that there is a genuine source of authority. In Pascal's notebook of assorted thoughts there is this observation: "Men like certainty. They like the Pope to be infallible in faith, and grave doctors to be infallible in morals, so as to have certainty." He meant by "doctors" the academic doctors. We would want to add that we want infallibility from our physicians. But we are desperate because we find no infallible authority among men for faith, government, philosophy, medicine, economics, or any other area of life. There are no unimpeachable sources or accurate, trustworthy fortune-tellers. And there never will be an infallible source of authority in human flesh . . . except one. And

He Understands Me!

that is Jesus Christ.

He is the one—and the only one—who holds before us a standard of right and wrong which is trustworthy; who demands our best efforts; who will call into question our ethical catastrophes, our dishonest intentions, or our demeaning attitudes.

For some time now our nation has enjoyed escaping authority. It has appeared exciting and amusing to throw out the rules. But now that we don't know who can be trusted and all facets of our future are in doubt, we are realizing the trauma of an authority crisis. America of the seventies will call "good news" what America of the sixties called a repressive heresy. That heresy-turned-gospel is the existence of a viable authority figure. And the authority figure, who is he? God our Father as represented and communicated to us through his Son, our Brother, Jesus the carpenter from—where was it?

A second message from the Master Communicator is a word of assurance. Jesus acknowledged and affirmed Nathanael as a genuine Israelite. He heard the deep things rumbling in that man's mind, and he assured him that he was heard and that it mattered what he felt and thought. That kind of assurance is good news, too. Isn't it helpful to know that someone cares about our frustrating efforts to bring some good into this world? Haven't you wondered whether virtue was a lost cause? Haven't you agonized over the difference between the palace you had hoped to create and the woodshed you finally built? Well the second word from Jesus is that he cares about those things which concern you deeply, and he would assure you that it makes a difference to him in the depth of his being what is going on in the depth of your being.

Their conversation about Nathanael being under the fig tree has prompted a few commentators to refer to the apocryphal story of Susanna who was accused of adultery under a tree. When the witnesses were asked separately to state under which tree the adultery took place, their answers were contradictory and thus their foul plot to smear Susanna's honor was foiled. It is pleasant to hear of a story where virtue is vindicated but our lives are usually more mundane. The temptations and accusations we face are seldom on a scale with the charge of adultery on the part of a nationally prominent figure. And quite often it appears that no one knows or cares at what points we are guilty or innocent. But what I am trying to say is that Jesus tells us he hears us.

That is good news!

The Civilized Christian

There was a man named Nicodemus, a leader of the Jews, who belonged to the party of the Pharisees. One night he came to Jesus. John 3:1-2

I recall seeing Peter Ustinov in the role of a Roman senator saying, "I have found it wise to acknowledge the gods publicly but to ignore them privately." The snickers from the audience indicated that they felt the same way. "You don't really believe in God, do you?" is the question of the sophisticated, civilized world. But the encounter of Jesus with Nicodemus shows us that Christian faith is for the civilized. Christianity is not a blind, empty religion. It is a faith suitable for those with probing minds. Belief is necessary for the dispossessed, but it is also possible and necessary for Nicodemus, Paul, Augustine, William Temple, and Paul Tillich.

Christianity has a place for the inquiring. It has a place for the man whose mind stretches, who is investigative and must know more than just the surface of life. It is night as Nicodemus comes to Jesus to ask questions. He is perplexed by what is happening among the people. He knows that Jesus is an effective teacher, but is he more? The third chapter of John lists a couple of his inquiries, perhaps there were other questions, but surely there is no question more pertinent nor more puzzling than his, "How can a grown man be born again?"

Nicodemus is a responsible teacher of the law. It is unique that an older, richer, educated Jew seeks counsel of a younger, poorer, unschooled Jew. Yet Jesus can claim a unique authority, wealth, and wisdom.

It is not a fallacy for intelligent minds to seek out Jesus Christ. It is not out of bounds in a rational sense to probe into the mysteries of this new teacher. To follow after an evangelist need not scandalize an inquiring mind. To be sure, the Bible can satisfy much of the hunger of an intellectual search. Someone has described the Bible as a stream where children can wade and elephants can swim.

The Bible speaks to us of the quality and the meaning of life. The expression "eternal Life" tells us that Jesus Christ, who is *the Life* can extend to us a rich and meaningful existence.

The Bible presents a unique message which is without parallel. Its accurate categorizing of sin and appealing offer of salvation is a challenge to the researching of an inquiring mind. Indeed, the Bible describes man in such a way that the reader is astonished at the accuracy of the description.

The effect of the biblical message can be an explosive display of hurricane power or a life-giving breezy freshness. The mark of the Holy Spirit upon individuals, upon society, upon history is worthy of the most serious study and will stand up under the severest rational scrutiny.

The biblical message is philosophically sound, it is logically sound, it is historically sound, it is psychologically sound. The biblical message can be attractively presented to an open mind. Thorough inquiry will see him as the Savior of mankind, the hope of the world.

It is not unreasonable to commit oneself to Jesus Christ in faith. To hold to faith presuppositions is an intelligent response; it is even a step in the scientific process. An hypothesis, necessary in any scientific investigation, is nothing more than a faith presupposition. If you accept the wind, why not

The Civilized Christian

accept the Spirit? Although you may know about the rotation of the earth, barometric pressure, temperature changes, and other causes of the wind, it does not follow that you have captured the secret of the wind. In the same way, you will never capture a full understanding of the Spirit, but you can still intelligently worship God.

You understand, I hope, that I am not attempting to reduce Christianity to a science nor am I trying to say that I can rationally convince you that Jesus Christ is the Son of God. My point is simply that there is room within Christianity for an inquiring mind.

When Albert Schweitzer was eight years old, his father gave him a New Testament. After reading in it, he returned to his father to ask, "What did Mary and Joseph do with the gold, frankinscence, and myrrh? Why were they so poor after this? What happened to the Wise Men? Why is nothing said of their becoming disciples?" Schweitzer applied his inquiring mind to everything he did. While studying for a Ph.D. in both theology and music, he wrote a monumental two-volume study of Bach and revolutionized the theory of Bach. He criticized the current changes in organ building and wrote *The Gospel of the Organ* which was finally accepted as the authoritative work on organs. His in-depth study of Immanuel Kant was a revelation to those most familiar with that philosopher. He rotated as organist and preacher in the church where he served. At the age of twenty-six he was the principal of the school of theology at Strasbourg. His *Quest for the Historical Jesus* turned the theological world upside down. In his mid-thirties he received a medical degree and then astounded the world by establishing a medical mission work in Africa.

Someone has written of Schweitzer:

> Albert Schweitzer, whose faith was better than his theology, and whose life was always better than whatever faith he confessed, will forever challenge and judge lesser men whose theologies are better than their faith and

whose lives are a poor second to their professions.

Christianity has room for such men with such minds. There need be no conflict between faith and reason. Albert Schweitzer was a genius, proven so in many different areas of thought, a man with an inquiring mind who pursued Jesus Christ.

Nicodemus appears in other places throughout John's Gospel. In John 7:50-51 we find him again. He chastens the Pharisees who boast that none of their number believe in Jesus. They crow that they are guardians of the law. But Nicodemus, himself a Pharisee, defends Jesus and criticizes their misuse of the law. The passage reads: "Nicodemus was one of them; he was the one who had gone to see Jesus before. He said to them, 'According to our Law we cannot condemn a man before hearing him and finding out what he has done.'" In other words, he demands of his colleagues that justice be found in the court of justice.

Nicodemus makes an appeal for fairness, and we observe that *Christianity has a place for the fair-minded.* Fairness (is that a traditional theological term?) is within the purposes of God. Jesus Christ did not come into this world to arbitrarily condemn the world. He came to bring light so that men could make a fair decision about God. He did not come to the establishment. He came to the outsiders so that everyone could have a fair chance at God. Jesus did not company with many of the elite; rather he appealed primarily to those who might be called the dregs of society. His life says to us that God is concerned to give everyone a fair chance. Men call God unfair because of hell. The better perspective is that God is providing everyone a fair opportunity for heaven. If Christianity is anything, it is a mandate for equity in society.

Of course equality needs a lot of definition. When I use the term, I think of Paul's description of a church where no one has the same gifts but all are equally important.

Justice is a significant present concern. A great many people are calling for equity in life. Those about us who are calling

The Civilized Christian

for fairness—either for themselves or others—should learn that Christianity is very much in agreement with a plea for fairness.

Reinhold Niebuhr was a young pastor in Detroit when that city grew tremendously following the First World War. As pastor of an auto workers congregation he felt their bitterness at being exploited. He knew how the factory system was depersonalizing them and, as a result, he waded into the social problems he saw by presiding at labor forums, by lecturing, and by denouncing Ford's millions held in reserve while workers starved. He once said, "The lowliest peasant of the Dark Ages had more opportunity for self-expression than the highest paid employee in the Ford factory." Do you see a relationship between inequity and iniquity? Are you concerned about fairness? Christ is too.

Let me point out another place in the Fourth Gospel where attention is given to Nicodemus. Reading from 19:38-40.

> After this, Joseph who was from the town of Arimathea, asked Pilate if he could take Jesus' body. (Joseph was a follower of Jesus, but in secret, because he was afraid of the Jews.) Pilate told him he could have the body, so Joseph went and took it away. Nicodemus, who at first had gone to see Jesus at night, went with Joseph, taking with him about one hundred pounds of spices, a mixture of myrrh and aloes. The two men took Jesus' body and wrapped it in linen cloths with the spices; for this is how the Jews prepare a body for burial.

At first blush this may appear a rather insignificant thing. But this is an account of a very courageous act, and we could well spend time speaking of Christian courage. However, I feel there is an even more significant character trait revealed here. This was a humane, compassionate thing to do.

Christianity has a place for the compassionate. It is true that there is a type of church member whose religion is just for him alone. This is that kind of man whose faith is hermetically sealed inside of him and none of his Christianity ever leaks out to drip on someone else. But we have not so learned Christ. Christianity is a compassionate faith.

Too often the compassionate humanist is opposed to the church. Humanism was a development of a classical and literary revival in fourteenth-century Italy. It held religious ideas in disdain. It was cynical about spiritual thought. This may have been the natural reaction to the Renaissance church, but it need not be so. One of humanism's brightest stars was Erasmus who attempted to refashion the church rather than reject it.

Christian history gives ample evidence that Christianity is compassionate. For instance, prison reform is thought to be a modern outbreaking of compassion; however, the history of prison reform actually begins with the story of John Howard, an English Baptist layman. Howard inherited a fortune in 1742 and proceeded to see the world. While on his way to Lisbon, he was captured by a French pirate and imprisoned under terrible conditions.

Howard, because of his influence, was allowed to return to England where in 1773 he was elected high sheriff of Bedford County. Remembering his own imprisonment, Howard investigated the prison system under his authority. The high sheriff was appalled by the prison conditions. The worst practice was not paying jailers who, in turn, maintained themselves at the prisoners' expense.

Because he was independently wealthy, Howard was able to travel extensively and observe the conditions of prisons in other countries. His methods of procedure were similar to those of a scientist doing a case study. From his observations and careful notes he published *The State of the Prisons in England and Wales, with Some Account of Foreign Prisons.*

Two bills resulting from his work were passed by Parliament within a year. Most of the prison reform of the next thirty years was due to the work of this one man. Howard traveled more than forty thousand miles and spent more than $120,000 of his own money working for prison reform. When Parliament passed prison reform laws, he paid to have them printed and mailed to every warden and prisonkeeper in England.

Compassion is not foreign to the faith of the Messiah. There is no greater compassion than God's compassion. He heard the cry of slaves in Egypt, and the weeping of Jeremiah, and knew a greater heartache than Hosea. While we were yet in our sins, God loved us and sent his Son. How can you fail to hear the compassion in the voice of Jesus calling: "Jerusalem, Jerusalem the city that murders the prophets and stones the messengers sent to her! How often have I longed to gather your children, as a hen gathers her brood under her wings; but you would not let me." The heart of the gospel is found in the compassionate heart of God.

But now let me put a new twist to what I have been saying. Christianity does more than just accept the inquiring, the fair-minded, and the compassionate. Christ-within is a catalyst that creates inquiry, that prompts a search for justice, and produces a well of compassion. Christianity is not so much a haven for the open-minded as it is a mind opener.

The basic ingredient needed in any life—for the civilized or the uncivilized— is *you must be born again!* The new man in Christ Jesus finds that his new spiritual dimension preserves the positive qualities of life. And he finds a new and deeper quality of life.

Arnold Toynbee in *An Historian's Approach to Religion* tells of the man-achieved beauty of Los Angeles where the vacant lots return to the desert. Whatever achievements are the possession of man, apart from God his tendency is downward.

Bring your desires and your fears, your questions and your doubts, your dreams and your nightmares to Jesus Christ and discover God's hurricane power, God's breeze-like refreshment— discover that you will be better for it.

Significant Living

Come and see the man who told me everything I have ever done. Could he be the Messiah?
John 4:28-29

One Saturday afternoon our family went looking for mountains in Nacogdoches County, Texas. East Texas is hilly country, but the natives like to refer to some of the higher hills as mountains. So we rode into the country until we could see something rising higher than the trees on the side of the road, and we turned off the farm-to-market road to find an East Texas mountain. The six-year-old in the back seat kept reciting: "We're going to get lost! We're going to get lost!" But we never got too far from a sleepy village located near the mountain.

Finding a place to leave the car was no problem. We quickly began a trek up the hillside. On the way up the hill our two-year-old discovered a hollow log which surely must have been a rabbit's home; so we spent the rest of the day talking about the rabbit tree.

The setting was a good place for a story. We could imagine that the immediate vicinity had been settled long ago (as, indeed, East Texas was) by a man named Jacob. This particular hill had been given to his son Josef and not far from the hill was a small town called Sychar (much like the village we had passed). At the top of the hill (if we can ever get there, what with chasing rabbits) is an old well dug by the great ancestor Jacob. The pure spring water is the best you have ever tasted.

Look down the hill and you will see someone—she looks to be an older woman from her posture, but I'll give you this much of a clue: she isn't as old as she looks. Wouldn't you say that she is poor because, if she had any money, she would have thicker clothing wrapped about her against this cold, crisp, clear January day. And isn't it peculiar that she comes to the well alone?

She comes to the well alone because the other women of the village will have nothing to do with her. This is a woman who, at one time or other, has been sister-in-law to everyone in town. She has had five different husbands and none of the marriages have worked.

Have you any idea what it might be like to live in a small town and to have been married five different times? Someone has called her "the woman of the shattered romances." Well, that is hard to see. Is there any romance to be shattered in five desperate liasons? Each time she hopes for the best but lives through the worst. Life shatters at the touch, and the neighbors—always a different set of neighbors, and yet not so different—the neighbors chatter again what they have been gossipping across back fences before.

How many children has the woman borne? Does she know? Does she contend with a six-year-old's directions or a two-year-old's imagination? Maybe you would rather not speculate on the way her existence has crumbled about her.

After—how many husbands was it?—anyway, she now has taken up with some fellow who just blew into town. She has no real idea who he is except that he is a warm body on cold nights. One of the ex-in-laws will say it just isn't right. But what does "right" mean to her?

Well, anyway, she is almost to the top. Everyday the hill gets higher and that pot gets heavier. At the top now, she starts to draw the water from one hundred feet below. Did you hear that? She is muttering something about a god who would fiendishly design underground water that runs under hills instead of through valleys. She almost has the water to the top when she realizes that she is not alone. You see, it so happens that the hill forms an intersection of highways; so it is not uncommon for travelers to stop by the well. As she pulls the sloshing water toward her, the stranger asks for a drink.

He's a Jew! You can tell it by his speech. For the first time she looks at him. Yes, a Jew! Now that is unusual. Jews never come through Samaria. And isn't that just like them! He waits until a lowly Samaritan comes along to draw his water.

"How come a Jew asks for a drink from a Samaritan woman? Don't you know that Jews are too good for Samaritans?" Ha! She is not about to give him a drink.

Evidently he is one of those middle-class-sheltered-momma's boys who expects everyone to be polite and "yes sir" him. He hasn't learned about the dog-eat-dog violence of this world so he responds, "If you had known who I am, you would have asked me for water."

That is silly. And she knows it is silly. There is no sense taking guff from a smart-aleck Jew so she says to him: "What are you going to do? Do you own a well? You haven't even got a bucket, how are you going to get me a drink from a hundred feet down? Are you a better man than Jacob who dug this well?"

The very idea! He was going to give her a drink. He didn't have anything to give her.

But the stranger still thinks that he has something to offer. The stranger says to her: "If you drink the water that you have there in that bucket, you are going to get thirsty again. But if you drink the water I give you, you won't get thirsty till kingdom come. The water I give is like a fountain of youth."

Oh brother! And he is so serious. Well now, you have to go along with someone like this because you never know when they might get violent.

"Okay, so give me a drink already."

That must have stumped him because he changes the subject. Or maybe he wants witnesses to see that he can get water out of a well without a bucket. Either way he says, "Go get your husband."

Of all the nerve! Some people really ask for it.

"I haven't got a husband!" she snaps.

"That's quite right. You have had five husbands and you have no legal ties to the man you are living with now. You certainly spoke the truth."

She could bite her tongue. "Evidently you must be a preacher," she says. What is so obvious about it I am still not certain, but she does know how to handle ministers.

"I just don't believe quite like you do."

This is supposed to be a witness-stopper. "I don't swallow once-saved-always-saved." End of discussion. "If baptism doesn't save you, then it looks like to me that sprinkling is just as good." Any statement will do that says there is no use arguing about doctrinal differences. Such a comment will usually serve to squelch the itinerant evangelist.

But this man will not be put off so easily. He responds, "It really doesn't make that much difference about the building in which you worship." (He really is a queer duck.) "The important thing is to recognize that God is a spiritual being and he must be worshiped in the reality of the spiritual realm."

Well this goes beyond her. But her instincts are still good. She has suffered with enough good sisters who wanted to save her in the past. She knows that now is the time to say something ecumenical like, "We are all striving for the same goal," and then split. She reaches for the water pot.

"Yeah, I know the Messiah will come one of these days and straighten out all our differences when he talks to us."

Significant Living

The stranger's words stop her cold.

"I am he, and I am talking to you now."

Have you ever been awakened by having cold water thrown in your face? It could not possibly be more of a shock than she received. It would be like receiving two letters in the mail, one a check for an income tax return of $300 and the other your draft notice. You wouldn't know whether to laugh or cry. Here she has been making those snappy remarks to the Messiah. Horrible! And yet wonderful! He is the one awaited by every Samaritan and Jew and here on this lonely hill he is talking to her. Judgment and joy mingle together.

About this time a dozen or so Jews clamber toward the well. It is all too much. Forgetting the water pot, she rushes into the village to tell somebody, anybody.

Again the Fourth Gospel has presented us a flesh and blood person meeting the Savior. In the encounter of the Samaritan woman with Jesus we see that *Christ offers significance to the sinner.* This woman had a thirst which was unrecognized. Jesus revealed her thirst and offered her a drink which would give her "the life of the age." That is literally what he said to her. The expression refers to the messianic age. Perhaps you might understand it better if the phrase were rendered "heavenly life"; that is, life like there is in heaven. New Testament translators call it eternal life, but that brings to mind something that goes on and on forever. That isn't wrong but it misses an important emphasis. The point is that Jesus was talking about life that has quality, significance.

If you happen to live in a dump with a gigolo whose name has escaped you for the moment, if you are number last in everyone's roster, if you are the crowned queen of trash—then significance is something you lack. That offer you can't refuse. A recent news item from Florida reflected this understanding. It seems that a teenager there remarked, "I know I'm somebody 'cause God don't make no junk!"

The offer that Jesus gives of significance is *a personal offer.*

Wouldn't you like to be known as more than a Social Security number? Throughout his life Jesus presented the same gospel to many different people, but he always considered their differences. She is a Samaritan, a woman, an outcast. She is a person deeply hidden behind the callouses on her soul. With others Jesus is tender but with her he must use a needle to prick through the thick hide down to where there is still some sensitivity.

Significant life is not a mass-produced commodity. Remember the words "Take my yoke and put it on you," came from a master carpenter who could fashion each yoke to the individual set of shoulders. Significant life is hand-crafted for you.

Significant life is life that has been therapeutically *purged*. The woman of Sychar had made a mess of her life. She couldn straighten it out on her own. She could not stop the awful trend of always goofing up her chances.

Significant living would mean for her that she had found an antidote for her personal problems and could learn to cope with a society that used her without regard or sympathy for her. You must, in some cases, learn your own significance apart from what society believes about you. The community may be slow to say you are important, or they may never admit it. But "everyone who believes in him" finds significance.

This offer of significance is also a *permanent* offer. One of the remarks Jesus makes to the woman sounds confusing. He offers a drink that does away with thirst. The woman wants such a drink so that she can forget about climbing that hill. But she misunderstands the man. And a goodly company of those who think they understand have misunderstood. Some who read this story think that salvation is a case of one dose and that is all. Walk down that aisle once and then you can forget about religion after that; you have settled it.

The water of life is not a spring that once tasted is forgotten One taste of salvation will do for the rest of life, however, because it becomes an artesian well continually flowing within.

Significant Living

One way to describe it would be to call it a fountain of youth. Even though the body may grow old, the spirit bathed in Christ remains forever young.

Maybe the most important point in the story is that Jesus' offer of significant life is a *present reality*.

We will put off theology for a better day. Today is the day for toting water from the well and scrubbing floors and washing windows. Now is the time for earning the rent, and bull sessions about pie-in-the-sky-bye-and-bye can wait!

Can it? What about questions like, "Does any of this make sense?" "Does anyone care about me?" "What am I supposed to do with my life?" These are questions for today. Salvation and significant living are not retirement hobbies. Clearing out the cobwebs of mind and soul are proper housecleaning chores for today.

Minority groups are calling for equality *now!* Environmentalists are saying that we must act *now* if our world is to have any future. Significant life is a quality Christians must discover and share *now!*

What Jesus has to say to the woman requires a response at that moment. And respond she did. With the wisdom of the injured who has been the butt of too many jokes, she runs into town and asks, "Do you suppose this stranger could be the Messiah?"

Her question sends the villagers out to invite that *Jew* to spend two nights in a *Samaritan* hamlet. Wow! Something significant must have happened.

"Ah, yes, some day the Messiah will come and we shall have a pleasant chat about this or that." No, the Messiah is attempting to break into your life now! For this moment consider the mass of people moving up and down hill, filling and emptying pots, never pausing for real refreshment. Right now, as you stumble through the mundane tasks of your existence, don't you wish for significant life?

No Cheap Tricks

The man believed. ... He and all his family believed.   John 4:50,53

A man pursues and is pursued. With a burning wish before him and anxious fears behind he climbs across the Galilean hills up twenty plus miles to Cana and then back again down to the Sea of Galilee and home where a shimmering image of hope beckons him.

Few stories illustrate such variety of meanings of the word "faith." Faith is a precious commodity. The ability to believe—have I lost it entirely? How can people recite a list of miracles and smugly presume to have settled something? The substitute lamb for Isaac, the whole Exodus experience, the conquest of Canaan, the return of the captives from Babylon—I know those events. That man who fed the crowds and healed the dregs of society from their filthy diseases is known also. I know the astounding cosmic tricks which are supposed to have been performed. What I would like to know is why?

Therefore I am surprised and pleased by the way this scurrying government official is greeted. Oh, it seems a bit calloused, I admit, but I like it nonetheless. The man wants a quick miracle, it seems, as though this is bargain-basement day. Jesus cuts him short and the whole rank of miracle-mongers queuing up behind him. "You have to have your *wonders* before you will trust me, don't you." Too bad there is no plural "ye" in modern English to show how he shotgunned the whole array of skeptics and circus followers. The skeptics are those conservative religionists who will not vary the number of hymns in a midweek devotional meeting without putting out Gideon's fleece at least once more than Gideon himself did. The circus gallery is the rest of us who are not so serious about matters of piety or anything else for that matter. Entertainment! that's the good word—and the only one we know.

The circus crowd is usually out of place by their quest for the bizarre in the presence of the sublime. Consider Jerome Bosch's painting *Christ Bearing the Cross.* The center of the painting is the pathetic, tragic figure of a man weighted down by a heavy cross and bearing on his forehead a piercing crown of thorns. A soldier leans heavily upon the cross increasing the burden. A mob presses about him but none look directly at the central figure and no one observes or contemplates the tragedy. They are near animals thirsty for blood. The cartoon-like quality of Bosch's characters speaks of an entertainment-based existence. The kill is what they want—or a miracle. Make the event bloody or spectacular, preferably both. If Jesus would leap off the cross with a full somersault, that would be stupendous! colossal!

Jesus meant to stop this kind of miracle-mongering before it got far. Our story includes the only use of the term "wonders" in the book of John and it is used in a derogatory sense. No cheap miracles today!

And that should have turned the lot of them around; but not our anxious father from Capernaum. He did not come for any cheap miracles. In a few words and a look that filled in any gaps in his story, the man unmasks his agonizing love for an ill child. "Sir, come with me before my child dies." Jesus responds with equal compassion, brevity, and straightforwardness: "Go, your son will live!" And because Jesus

No Cheap Tricks

seems believable, the man hurries home.

You mean to say that he practically broke his neck galloping across those hills in a frenzy over his boy for five short words!

Well, can you think of anything else he would rather have heard? Jesus said precisely what the man needed to hear.

But didn't Jesus just finish saying something negative about crowd-pleasing, skeptic-squelching "wonders."

As a matter of fact he did. Which brings up the whole question of miracles and their purpose. There are two illusive questions to ask of this and any other miracle. They are important questions and must be asked but yield only partial and unsatisfactory (at least to me) answers. The first question is, *What happened?* In this case the child got well; the father and the family believed. Evidentally Jesus exercised power and compassion in a word or thought. However, the simple statement of events—word, cure, belief—does not necessarily indicate cause-and-effect relationship. This question and answer will not satisfy our curiosity about the matter.

The second question is, *How did it happen?* This question gives the opportunity to join the events and say the word caused the cure caused the belief. This answer will be all that some desire of the storyteller. But it still seems incomplete to me. It is sufficient, I suppose, for the principles in the story; but the answers to what and how leave me out of the story. I am not yet involved and so only partially interested.

A third and more significant question would be, *What does it mean?* In this case it meant that the child lived and that the family came to a new understanding of life. It means that Jesus is an exceptional person worthy of an exceptional kind of confidence. The explanation of the meaning of the miracle certainly speaks for the principles; but it speaks to me as well. You see when I ask the question of meaning I imply the question, "What does it mean to me?"

Significance is an important concept in the Fourth Gospel.

Jesus chides the crowd for wanting signs and wonders. As I have said, this is the only use of the word "wonders" in John's Gospel. The expression is a challenge to the crowd to reassess their opinions about fancy sleight-of-hand. The word "signs" is picked up by the author and used several times to make a point about the significance or meaning of what Jesus is doing. Miracles, mighty works, signs—whatever you choose to call them—they point back to Jesus to explain some things about the man and his ministry.

What do you learn about a man who can say, "Go, your son will live!" and at that moment, twenty miles away, the boy recuperates? Well obviously you can say he is powerful. And beyond that you can say that he is compassionate.

By bringing out the significance of what Jesus was doing so that we see such things as his power and compassion, the author is using these signs to elicit faith. Faith is what we find in this distraught father. In the presence of the Great Physician he accepted the Lord's short statement as true. He trusted Jesus on an immediate and personal level. Later, with his son, which is to say in the presence of the completed work of that Physician, he trusted on a profound yet no less personal level.

The story of this man's mental and spiritual experience leads me to conclude that *insight and faith are reciprocal catalysts.* Let me attempt to shed some light on what I am trying to say. A catalyst facilitates a new experience. It speeds up a happening. Here Jesus is establishing a growing relationship with this man. The man exercises faith. The faith accelerates the rate of the relationship's growth and leads to insight. The insight rapidly leads to a more intense kind of faith. Or, another way to put it would be to say that awareness led to hope, hope to information, information to trust, trust to knowledge, knowledge to confidence, and confidence to understanding.

Of course it is not always this way. And I must be careful

No Cheap Tricks

to say that insight and faith are entirely different modes of relating to personalities and experiences. You can have faith without insight as in those tragic instances where the child dies and no one understands, but a father or mother continues to cling to a primary trust in God. And you can have insight without faith as in those appreciated occasions where the child lives due to medical genius, but no one gives the slightest thought to the spiritual implications of our patterns of life and death.

Insight is not faith. Faith is not insight. But each one has a way of bringing the other to maturity.

It appears to be a major concern of the Evangelist to join insight and faith. For those who see, belief is possible. For those who believe, perception is possible. Those who neither see nor believe are the skeptics and the circus crowd. Unfortunately the one has no ability to trust anyone and the other has no capacity for understanding.

Jesus made a gallant effort in his first remark to shake them into some glimmer of awareness, to bring a particle of hope into their closed systems. But only the man who had brought a newly expanding awareness and a desperate hope with him stood ready to trust and to learn.

The Man or the System?

Jesus said to him, "Get up, pick up your mat, and walk." Immediately the man got well; he picked up his mat, and walked. The day this happened was a Sabbath. John 5:8-9

Here is a case of rules getting in the way of helping people. A man calls for help but he is not to be answered because of the rules. In this case the rules say only emergency medical treatment on the sabbath. This man has been lame for thirty-eight years. And the religious system protectors are quick to point out that the system has no room for sabbath healings. Certainly it would have been very easy just to come back the next day and heal the man.

Jesus uses the occasion to expose the tendency of religious systems. Religious systems begin with a radical affirmation of God and man and then tend away from both God and man toward an affirmation of the system itself. Maybe this is what Dr. T. B. Maston meant when he said that Southern Baptists are more southern than Baptist and more Baptist than Christian.

This may explain why a denomination, like for instance the Catholics, can house both St. Francis of Assissi and the Spanish Inquisition. Or why Baptists can affirm the freedom of the believer in a statement on individual priesthood but can also suffer large breeches in fellowship when that freedom is exercised in incidental areas. It may explain why one man like Ulrich Zwingli can come to a vibrant understanding of the meaning of the Lord's Supper but eventually would persecute Anabaptists who threatened his system. A good beginning based on personal values often deteriorates into a morass of system values.

Do you remember Ivan's story of the Grand Inquisitor in *The Brothers Karamazov?* Ivan tells his younger brother a legend about Jesus returning to Seville, Spain, at the height of the Inquisition. He is popularly received until the Grand Inquisitor, who happened to have burned a hundred heretics the day before, has Jesus thrown in prison. He stands before Jesus and tells him he has no right to come back because everything is now in the church's hands. He tells Jesus that the church has corrected his work by making men slaves of the church. They both are silent, and then Jesus kisses the ninety-year-old inquisitor. The old man shudders, goes to the door, opens it and says, "Go, and come no more." Jesus is a system breaker.

In the midst of our systems we need a return to a Jesus perspective of people. The local church where I am a member is an incorporated body with material holdings. We have political and sociological standing in our community and country. We are quite jealous of our ecclesiastical involvements. They are our vested interests. Can we think in terms of people? We may think we are people conscious when we really see persons as potential pegs to fill organizational holes. Or we may see persons simply as financial spiggots to help fill up our leaky money bucket.

Commitment to God and to people makes one a radical. Commitment to a system makes one reactionary. It seems that all movements follow this path reading from left to right. Institutional rigor mortis sets in whether the system is Christianity or communism. Can we do anything to avoid it?

Yes, I think there is something we can do to thwart the

The Man or the System?

calcifying effect of time. The secret is not to avoid our development. The secret is to keep development in line with our first principles. In other words, let us never obscure a Jesus perspective. In John 5 Jesus says to this lame man, "I care about you." That is the Jesus perspective of people.

Jesus cared enough to personalize and particularize. Hear him. "Do you want to get well?" an unusual greeting. "Get up . . . walk," a direct challenge to the will. Jesus heals the man and then the religious leaders question him about his sabbath healing. The man knows nothing about the person who has effected a great change in his life, then he meets Jesus in the Temple and hears him say, "Quit your sins"—rather blunt counsel.

One thing that stands out in the book of John is the way that Jesus relates to different people as individuals. He understood that we are each one of a particular individual and any problem or difficulty is personal and unique.

What an outstanding trait this is! We tend to generalize people. People are herds of students, globs of faculty, or Aggies; they are blacks, browns, or Anglos. The Cheyenne Indians had the marvelous habit of calling themselves human beings; but they looked on the rest of humanity as something else. This is somewhat like the Jewish habit of dividing the world into the Jews and the nations—a word which has come to mean Gentiles, a synonym for leftover, second class.

It is amazing what changes can come to your life if you know that just one person cares personally and particularly about you. Dr. William Glasser contends that becoming involved with a client so that he senses your personal concern is one of the requirements for successful psychotherapy. In support of his point he tells of a couple who lived through the terrifying experience of an airplane crash in northern Canada. The two people survived forty-nine days in good health and good spirits even though they were without food. Both claimed to be sustained by the other person and by their faith in ultimate rescue.

Dr. Glasser says that psychiatry must be concerned with two basic psychological needs: *the need to love and be loved and the need to feel that we are worthwhile to ourselves and to others.*

Jesus showed his love for particular individuals. He certainly performed as a health-giving person. Centuries before the insights of modern psychiatry, Jesus was healing minds and bodies by living out the principles which men continually "rediscover." Glasser's first point about love is exemplified in Jesus' ability to particularize.

The second point states that we need to feel that we are worthwhile to ourselves and to others. Jesus was quite well aware of this, for *Jesus cared enough to challenge and discipline.* Listen again to the overtones of what he says to this man: You have been waited on as an invalid for a lifetime; do you really want to get well? You claim the need for assistance; would you take some initiative, exercise your will and stand up? And then later, in terms that will communicate to the man ("Quit your sins."), he warns him that being the recipient of healing does not release a man from the pitfalls of humanity. Newfound life and strength is not a license for irresponsibility.

It takes a genuine concern for a particular person to say to that one: I want you to do better and I want to help you do better. I want you to be the person you can be.

Dr. Glasser tells the story of Sharon who was confined to the Ventura School for girls in California for a number of delinquent offenses. At the school she disrupted the order of things and, at first, was not receptive to Dr. Glasser's reality therapy techniques. Dr. Glasser challenged Sharon to improve her behavior rather than bring upon herself severe disciplinary measures. Against what most of us would have expected, Sharon accepted the challenge and entered a therapy relationship which has seen her grow into a responsible young lady.

Dr. Glasser writes of Sharon: "Actually she had been looking for someone who was genuinely interested in her and who was tough enough to mean what he said." The doctor goes on to caution, "Patients want you to correct their irresponsible behavior, but they want it to be done in the genuine spirit of helping them, not to satisfy yourself by winning a power struggle."

Jesus fully satisfies this need. He cares enough to challenge and discipline.

Jesus also cared enough to risk the wrath of the system protectors. System protectors are all about us. In television, they champion copies of last year's hit but deny efforts at innovation. As alumni, they protect football while it bleeds the financial life out of a school. In politics, they guard the vested interests of a few old heads while progress seeks another community. In church, they keep a tight rein on all things dear and precious and shut out the fresh breeze of the Spirit. They guard the system; but they are, in fact, its worst enemies.

The system protectors misunderstand the nature of God. God is not a prisoner of any man's system. They are confused about the question of authority. Incorrectly, the system is identified with high authority and the protector-interpreter of the system becomes the highest authority.

When men commit themselves body and soul to a system, they become dangerous. And like Dostoevsky's Grand Inquisitor, they would kill Jesus Christ himself if he became a threat. Jesus risked himself by kicking the system. They killed Jesus but ultimately it is the system that fell.

Of course, we must be careful about throwing away rules. You could end up with a very fluid humanism that has no pole star. The anchoring point for a Jesus perspective is the vitality of personal contact with God and with man.

The late Rabbi Abraham Heschel advised:

> The central commandment is in relation to the person.
> But religion today has lost sight of the person.

Religion has become an impersonal affair, an institutional loyalty. It survives on the level of activities rather than in the stillness of commitment. It has fallen victim to the belief that the real is only that which can be registered by fact-finding surveys.

The institutional church may become preoccupied with oiling the machinery; but I can't believe that Jesus ever "lost sight of the person."

The Square Root of Blindness

One thing I do know: I was blind, and now I see.
John 9:25

Can you imagine a group of interns following a resident doctor across the lawn in the Medical Center of Houston when one of them says to their leader: "Sir, what is the square root of all the pain within a one mile radius?"

This is the same kind of question that the disciples ask of Jesus in John 9: "Teacher, whose sin was it that caused him to be born blind? His own or his parents' sin?" Perhaps the response of Jesus could be interpreted to say: "You just want to watch this life. Instead let us participate in this man's life."

That's a good suggestion for us as we attempt to gain something from the ninth chapter of John. Let's participate for a moment in the blind man's life. Evidently by wanting to participate in this man's life Jesus was offering a new kind of relationship to him. His neighbors couldn't even decide for sure whether or not he was the man they had always known. The religious leaders show that they are not interested in sharing the man's life; they simply want to preserve the fabric of their own system. Few of the people who composed this man's world were actively involved in his life.

As we move closer to the scene, notice the contrast in the

use of the expression "I know." These statements show the poor man to have a good grip on reality while the council is debating the square root of blindness.

The "blind" man is able to say honestly what he knows. It is simply this: a man made a paste and instructed him to wash it off and now he sees. The man frankly says: "I don't know where he is." "I think he is someone special." "I don't know if he is a sinner, but I do know that I was blind and now I can see." And then there is his cutting cleverness when he says, "It is amazing that you people who know everything don't know him."

On the other side is the arrogance of the council who knows all. "We know this man is a sinner." "We know Moses but we don't know where this man hails from." Don't fail to catch their implication, "We know religious truth but you know nothing."

There is also the pathetic timidity of the parents who say: "We know this is our son, and we know he was born blind, but we don't know anything that might get us into trouble."

And I have already mentioned the lack of observation on the part of those who say, "We don't know whether we know this fellow or not."

Several of John's themes coalesce in this one chapter. There are the themes of knowledge, the contrast of religionists and common people, and the theme of light and dark. There are overtones of the messianic theme of the exaltation of the humble in the story of the untrained blind man who can see spiritual truth more clearly than can the religiously skilled.

It is an amusing, cleverly told story—unless, of course, you make the mistake of sticking around too long so that you find yourself asking, "Am I blind?"

These are very simple questions—One either sees or does not see; one knows or does not know—and yet, it is so easy to raise a fog that makes everything dim and misty. The blind man knows a few simple experiences; he knows a man in a

The Squareroot of Blindness

limited relationship. It isn't much, but it is of considerably more value than what the experts know. The council is asking questions of conceptualization, perception, systematization, cognition. The blind man only sees and knows.

His knowledge is something personal. He knows a man, a relationship. He knows his own history, an experience. Although he can tell others about it, and he does many times, he cannot really share his knowledge. The kind of knowledge that the Pharisees want is conceptual. They want simple ideas and ideas can be shared. There is an important contrast here which has to do with you and how you know God or how you know any personality.

Someone asks: 'What is God like? Do you know God?" You might respond, "Plato said that God is the prime mover, the first cause." These are ideas. If you have a philosophical bent, you can appropriate an idea and think it with all the skill of a Greek. But does that mean you know God?

I can imagine our blind man saying, "Plato I know not, but Jesus I know." It is a very personal statement. It reminds me of Paul's unusual expression "according to my gospel." Now that is a hard phrase to understand if he means "my creedal statement" or "my outline of doctrine" or "my definition of the nature and attributes of God." But it makes good sense if Paul was saying what the words originally meant: "according to my good news."

Each of you has your own good news about God. Quite honestly, what does God mean to you personally? What is your good news? Someone might say, "I don't know about theology, but I do know that I can breathe now. I used to be very short-winded." It would be hard to work that into a systematic discussion of santification; but if that were your good news, it would be worth more to you than expertise in Tillichian thought.

I suppose it would be unnecessary to belabor the point that *his knowledge was held in humility.* It becomes him that he will not claim to know what he does not know. The religionists would have done well to ape him rather than despise him. None of us knows such a great lot about personal relationships, either in the spiritual realm or the social sphere. We would do well to admit "I know God and I know people and I know myself, but I know none of these too very well."

My point in all of this is not to say that theology or philosophy is wrong and out of place. The point is simply that participating in life through personal experience and personal relationships is primary, foundational. Without this kind of knowledge all other quasi-knowledge is nonsense.

We must be conscious of the dimension of personal experience. We bring our relationships and our personal histories with us to our theology and our rituals. And if our personal lives hold not a trace of knowledge of God and men, then our rituals will be stillborn, our theologies sterile.

We are often concerned about the old and the new in religious ritual—tradition versus innovation. Your personal faith and the display of that faith is the most vital consideration in anything you do in worship. The faith which was your ancestors informs you but it is not yours. If you do not experience God personally and uniquely, the precision of your ritual is meaningless.

Of course, the blind man who expresses his simple faith was not without significant tradition. The religious teachings of several generations had prepared him to hear Jesus ask, "Do you affirm the Son of man?" A healthy tradition allowed him to respond in faith even though the crusty tradition of the council would have stifled him. Actually they would have stifled the humanitarian action of Jesus; they would have prevented his healing on the sabbath.

If you want a systematic discussion of the hypotenuse of happiness, Jesus wasn't much of a Jew. I doubt that he would be accepted as fitting into many a Christian system. But he knew people.

Do you know him?

The Realist and the Mystic

They had prepared a dinner for him there, and Martha helped serve it, while Lazarus sat at the table with Jesus. Then Mary took a whole pint of a very expensive perfume made of nard, poured it on Jesus' feet, and wiped them with her hair. The sweet smell of the perfume filled the whole house.
John 12:2-3

There are three different passages in the New Testament that talk about Mary and Martha; the third of these is found in John 12. Jesus is the chief guest at a celebration in the home of Mary, Martha, and Lazarus.

In this special occasion together, the sisters are quite aware of one of the recent events found in John 11: the raising of Lazarus. The scene in John 12—Martha serving in the kitchen contrasted with what Mary is doing and what someone else wants her to have done—is also reminiscent of that occasion described in Luke 10 when Jesus visited in their home. Then Martha was working in the kitchen while Mary sat at Jesus' feet.

These two sisters contrast considerably. I call them the realist and the mystic; I guess that's as good a description as any. Martha is a very practical person and sees everything in practical terms. She sees life in terms of housekeeping and meals to be prepared. Mary is a very meditative person.

I'm very glad that they are sisters, because it would be so easy to find a contrasting husband and wife and use such a couple as a paradigm for a discussion of masculine characteristics and feminine characteristics and—well, I wouldn't like to make everybody angry in telling one story.

Recently someone has written that men talk about the philosophical aspects of life and women talk about the personal aspects. People can be divided this way, but it isn't necessarily because they are male or female. So I am glad that these are sisters who contrast both in their lives and particularly in the way they relate to Jesus. This is the thing that I want you to see. Although these sisters are quite different, both are loved by Jesus, both of them have an important relationship with him.

As background for the Fourth Gospel's presentation of these sisters, consider that Luke's story shows *Jesus as companion for both of them.* Jesus and his disciples are in Bethany. How their friendship first begins we don't know, but Martha comes to know Jesus and his companions and invites them into her home for a meal. When they come to the house, she is found bustling about in the kitchen. This is her makeup, to be involved in the pots and pans. So if she is to express love to Jesus, the way she does it is to get into the kitchen and prepare him a meal. The spirit of this woman has been captured in this poem prayer:

> Lord of all pots and pans and things,
> Since I've no time to be
> A saint by doing lovely things,
> Or watching late with Thee,
> Or dreaming in the dawnlight,
> Or storming heaven's gates,
> Make me a saint by getting meals
> and washing up the plates.

Well, this is Martha. Sometimes the practical person looks at the meditative person and says, "Now I get things done while you just daydream." In fact, in the story, Martha comes out of the kitchen and says, "Well, don't you care that I'm doing all the work? Make Mary come in the kitchen." We

The Realist and the Mystic

really don't have room for the dreamers, the meditative, for those who want just to sit for a minute and think. It's interesting how many places you can find a sign on the wall that says, "THINK!" But if you look around, you will see no one is paying attention to the sign. We don't have time for thinkers or meditators; we must be busy doing things.

Perhaps there is too little sympathy for the meditative; on the other hand, it would be easy to be overly critical of Martha. William Barclay says that Martha is being kind in the wrong way. Jesus is in his last days. He is on his way to Calvary, and she is being busy, but this isn't what he needs. He needs somebody to sit with him and think. Well, I don't agree, I think that's an overstatement, an oversimplification. Isn't it possible that Jesus found some comfort in just hearing the hum of a home, in knowing that Martha is out there. Yes, he received comfort from Mary's presence but also from Martha.

We are not aware of the radical secularity of Jesus. How much he was a part of his world! We see him as a guru, as a "Religious Person." Yet Jesus was about the most unreligious person, in that capital "R" sense, that you would know. He was a man involved with his world, a man who could appreciate the common elements of life. And he probably gained something from the smell of cooking, the clatter of kitchen utensils, and whatever is involved in the noises of the home. Surely Martha had a ministry to Jesus.

Jesus is a companion to all kinds of people: people in kitchens, people in gardens, and people in shops. Jesus would have been concerned about the vignettes of life, like a piano recital. He told stories about the common things of life. He didn't tell stories about two preachers on the way to a convention and how they witnessed to the stewardess on the plane. He told stories about a rascal who discovered a neighbor was gone so he stole into his garden and planted weeds while the neighbor was away. He told stories about people who could be recognized by someone not in the religious framework.

And he had a companionship with Martha that is not simply defined in religious terms.

Now the point of the story is not that he said to Martha, "You're wrong and Mary is right." What Jesus said to Martha was, "You have your way to communicate with me and Mary has hers, let her alone."

There are some people who would say to you, "I love you and here is some fruit that I canned." Somebody else would say to you, "I love you and let's sit and talk." And you can't say one is right and the other is wrong.

In our home we have been concerned about the hostess image that is coming through to our children. Should a hostess fix sandwiches and spend her time with her guests or prepare sumptuous meals and spend her time in the kitchen? We have always felt like it was more important for a hostess to be with the guests. Now we're not so sure. Some people don't communicate that way. Some people communicate by five different kinds of vegetables. Some people communicate by saying, "Let's go some place together." And either is right if it is a natural expression of who you are.

It is tragic when people do not understand love when it is communicated to them. Thomas Carlyle was said to have loved Jane Walsh Carlyle very much. But he was a cross-grained, irritable old codger. He made her life miserable. Then she died suddenly. Carlyle was supposed to have said, "I wish I could have her back for just five minutes, to tell her how much I have loved her through all of this that I have put her through. She never knew it. Never." Now that is a terrible thing when people live together and have not learned to be companions who know how to communicate with one another.

Jesus is exceptionally one who is able to be a companion, one who is able to communicate with you and understand your distinctive way of communicating. Whether you are one who says, "I want to be teacher of a class, and I want to lead

The Realist and the Mystic

Junior boys to the Lord," or whether you are one who says, "I know how to trim the hedges and mow the yard," Jesus is able to be a companion to you.

With that introduction to Jesus' relationship with the sisters, let us look at the story in John 11 where we find *Jesus as comforter for both of them* and it must be a different kind of comfort for each one of them. You know the story. The disciples receive a note that Lazarus is sick. Augustine comments that the message they send doesn't say, "Please come." It just says he is sick. Augustine felt that this is all they needed to say. It is not possible for a man both to love a friend and desert him at the same time. They know all they have to do is let Jesus know Lazarus is sick and he will come. Yet, for some strange reason, that isn't what happens. The disciples don't understand. Mysteriously, Jesus says it is all going to work out for the glory of God. How can that be when they arrive too late to see their friend alive?

Now Martha, the very practical one, hears that he is coming. She leaves the group of mourners to go speak to Jesus because it would have been improper for Jesus and Martha to talk in the midst of this group, for the most part men, who had been mourning. So Martha goes to meet him halfway. Much like the slighted mother, she scolds him. "The rabbi business isn't so good you couldn't have phoned? Why didn't you come?" And yet, with a feeling of complete confidence, she says, "I know you could have done anything, and I know you now can take care of the situation." It is necessary for Jesus to answer hard practical questions.

"Why has this happened?"

"You believe, don't you, in the resurrection of the dead?"

"Yes, I do, that's the orthodox belief."

"Well, you must understand that I am the resurrection and the life."

There is a theological discussion near the grave of this departed brother. And that's the way to treat Martha. In this passage we have one of the high points of Jesus' discourses.

Martha returns and says, "Mary, the Lord is here; he wants to talk to you." Mary comes out and says almost word for word exactly what Martha said except she falls to her knees and sobs it out. Jesus does not explain to her, "Now then, you must understand the doctrine of the resurrection of the dead." No, instead he groans, he suffers some very strong emotion—and there are numerous arguments about what the emotion is and what it means, but this is not a part of the passage to be explained. The part of the passage to be explained is where he is talking to Martha about the theology of death— this is a passage to be felt. He groans and he moans and he weeps and those who follow Mary say, "My didn't he love them" And this is the way to comfort Mary. This passage is one of the high points in the life of Jesus where we touch something of his feeling.

If you have participated in many funerals or have comforted many bereaved, you know that people handle grief in different ways. Someone says, "Why?" and to this person you must say, "Listen, you know that God is good and he comes into our lives to help us. You remember Psalm 116:15 tells us, 'How painful it is to the Lord when one of his people dies!' And you know what it says in Revelation 14:13, 'Happy are the dead who from now on die in the service of the Lord!' You have heard many times the twenty-third Psalm, 'Even if that way goes through deepest darkness, I will not be afraid, Lord, because you are with me!' You know that Jesus has told us he is the resurrection and the life. And you know from John 14 his promise that he is going to leave us to prepare mansions for us. You know this and there are so many things to be said about his coming back."

And the response is, "Yes, I know that. Thank you. That helps."

But yet someone else, maybe one of the members of that same family, will ask, "Why?" and with this one it is better

The Realist and the Mystic

not to come out with Scripture and theology. The answer is simply, "I don't know. But I hurt, too." The only real answer is simply, "I don't know. But I hurt, too." The only real answer is to share grief, to weep. Sometimes you will come away from a situation like this lamenting, "I didn't have anything to say; what can you say?" Then later your bereaved friend will greet you with, "Thank you for coming. You were so much help."

"How was I a help?"

"You were there."

Two different girls, quite different although they are sisters, and yet both responded to in such an excellent way by Jesus. So gifted was he to be able to see each person as unique. For anyone's grief, Jesus is a comfort.

The third of the instances where you see these sisters, the scene in their home described in John 12, points out that *Jesus is Christ to both of them.* After the raising of her brother, Martha opens their home for a properly organized party. And I can imagine that if Martha were among us today and someone were to say, "Look, Jesus is coming back," Martha would respond, "Well, that means we better get out the china and the crystal." Everything would have been done properly. All things would be in order and everything would be preceeded with proper statements of faith, doctrinally sound, carefully printed. This is Martha. She responds in a verbal way, a precise manner.

Now Mary comes. She comes with a frighteningly expensive jar of perfume and spills it all over Jesus. Then she undoes her hair and wipes his feet with her hair. This is a shocking thing to do because, you see, a proper woman would have her hair bound up. To wear your hair loose in society would indicate that more than just your hair was loose. It would indicate that your character was suspect. She comes with an abandon in a nonverbal way. She doesn't know what to say and is not good at words. She just pours her perfume all over him and wipes his feet in an act of love. It is both a solemn act of preparing for his burial and a joyous act expressing her love. In an act of abandonment, which Judas cannot tolerate, she expresses her feelings about Jesus.

While a college student, I was surprised by a professor's description of his conversion. He is a very reserved man who is not given to emotional display; however, as a young boy he was saved in an emotional experience. He cried and sobbed and vented a lot of feeling. As a result, he says that when somebody quietly walks down the aisle and calmly says, "I've accepted the Lord and I want to be a member of this church," he finds that difficult to accept. It is difficult for him to understand that anybody else could come to know Jesus without the excruitiating pain that he knew.

Fortunately, Jesus doesn't demand that we follow someone else's model. There is room for Martha, there is room for Mary. There is room for each of us to express to God either in a quiet, well-thought out, deliberately spoken way or in exploding emotion what we feel about him.

The book of John is full of double meanings and one can be found in chapter 12. John wrote that the perfume filled the whole house, which is typical of the way the Fourth Gospel is written. One can imagine that the whole house was filled with this expression of love. And, I suppose, if you happened to be sitting about halfway in between where Jesus was and where the kitchen was, you would have had a pleasant mingling of the perfume of Mary's joy and the kitchen odors of Martha's cooking. I think it would have been a pleasant place to be.

Two different sets of eyes, two different lives here, two different ways of seeing what Jesus meant to them—what an insight we get into Jesus as we are able to see his ability to be companion, comforter, and Lord to any life, whosoever it is.

A Family Affair

Not even his brothers believed in him.   John 7:5

On Sesame Street there is a routine where four muppets play father, mother, sister, brother and sing about their family. The four change costumes, wigs, and roles for a humorous effect and sing about their "perfectly ordinary, ordinarily perfect family." They give the impression of enjoying themselves at home.

The introduction to the family of Jesus in the Fourth Gospel shows them in a happy setting. His mother comes forward at a wedding celebration, apparently one of those who serve as auxiliary hostesses. At the end of the story we learn that other members of the family had been there, also. Meeting people at a wedding feast gives a pleasant image. From the various scraps of information which can be pieced together about this family, one has to be impressed that they enjoyed themselves at home.

Evidently Joseph was lost to them, but aside from that unfortunate circumstance the signs are good. They are a Galilean family. They are a trades family. The family is large enough to take care of one another but not too large. They would have been hardy people with a sound sense of values. The home would have been essentially religious without having a pompous or rigid air about it.

Here at the wedding feast Jesus first initiates his disciples into a sense of the dimensions of his ministry. His presence and action here would indicate that he is a man who enjoys life and would do his part to make a celebration a success.

But the story has overtones of tension. It is the story of a young man leading his companions into a new venture; but in order to do so there is some cutting of apron strings required.

The Fourth Gospel has three passages where Jesus is involved with his family. The wedding feast at Cana in chapter 2, the debate with the brothers in chapter 7 over Jesus' attendance at the Passover in Jerusalem, and Jesus' remarks to his mother and the beloved disciple from the cross found in chapter 19 indicate something of the relationship between this man with a mission and his family.

What did the family think of Jesus? *They rejected his messiahship but respected his integrity.* Why did Mary inform Jesus that the wine was depleted? Obviously she had some confidence in him. Either she simply knew he would be concerned about their embarrassment, or she felt that his presence with his disciples helped cause the problem and she knew he would act responsibly, or she knew him to be resourceful and felt that he would help meet the crisis of the moment. There are a variety of explanations but they all hinge on Mary's confidence in her son. Her statement to the servants says this. She tells them in effect: "Do what he tells you. You can trust his judgment. I certainly do."

None of this means necessarily that his mother came to him with a request for a miracle. Those who knew him during his years of reaching maturity had great confidence in the young man. They were impressed with him, but not to the point of thinking him unique. Arthur John Gossip notes the strangeness of the fact that no one in his home town took his ministry seriously.

A Family Affair

The brothers insist that he should go to Jerusalem and openly display himself before the holiday crowd. The Temple at Passover time was much like a modern shopping center during the Christmas rush. A great crowd would be there. The brothers are sure that Jesus could impress a large number of people to become his disciples. They themselves will not be his followers, but it is because of a lack of belief not a lack of respect.

There are always those charlatans about who cannot elicit the support of those who know them too well. Friends and family may acknowledge relationship—some frauds are really quite likeable; yet they are not believable because they lack integrity. But this is not the case with Jesus. Those who knew him best knew him to be sincere, honest, straightforward. Their lack of belief was not because his life contradicted his claims. It was simply that familiar family incredulity: "My boy makes me proud, but he couldn't be the president, or the king, or the Messiah."

It would seem curious that the brothers were not sufficiently awed by miracles to accept the claims of Jesus. Evidentally miracles in themselves do not lead to faith. The family may admit that Jesus can do wonderful things; but they do not believe because they do not understand the significance of those actions. The whole point of the Fourth Gospel seems to be to show the meaning behind the wonderful things we already have heard about Jesus.

To turn this discussion around, what did Jesus think of his family? *He rejected family pressures but accepted responsibility for their larger needs.* Some say he showed disrespect for his mother and lied to his brothers. Neither of these charges is true. In Cana Jesus used language that would have been proper for any male to direct toward a senior female. It was not disrespectful. It was, however, peculiar for a son to address his mother with, "Woman, what has that got to do with us?" Rather than disrespect, Jesus was proclaiming a new perspective for his mother. She and the remainder of the family must begin to think in terms of a new relationship with this man. Jesus wanted to take on a larger relation to them than son or brother.

Because the author never uses the name of anyone related to Jesus there is a subtle statement that his kin must transcend the blood relationships of the earthly family and discover the greater relations of the spiritual family. Jesus has called his disciples from their families and in turn he breaks from his own, not in the sense of renouncing them, but in order to accept them in a new relation as Lord and Savior.

The family tension shown in this Gospel is similar to the pain of maturing which many other young men have known. You can hear the plea: "I am no longer your little boy! Let go of me! Allow me to become a larger person!"

The brothers urge him to go to Jerusalem openly and Jesus says that it isn't the proper time for that. They leave and he goes to Jerusalem in spite of what he said. Did he lie to his brothers? No. The key is found in an expression used in both the scene at Cana and the confrontation with the brothers. As is true throughout this Gospel, an expression is used which has a profound double meaning. When Mary tells Jesus of the short supply of wine and when the brothers point out the anxious crowds in Jerusalem, Jesus responds, "This isn't the time." On the surface he appears to say: "Just hold on a moment. I'll act when there is a more opportune time." This understanding places the timing within the situation. Jesus appears to be saying that he will do what is expedient. But as the term is repeated throughout the Gospel it becomes clear that he is referring to a moment divinely set. Jesus does not refer to opportunism. He means instead redemption.

The brothers are going to Jerusalem and would like Jesus to go along and make a grand display. Jesus says no. He is not merely refusing to go along with them; he is refusing to destroy the rhythm of redemption. He does go to Jerusalem,

A Family Affair

but alone and unobtrusively. He refuses their simple request in order that he might fulfill their larger needs in God's time.

The brothers do not yet understand that his destiny is not popularity but hatred. Because they do not understand they are rebuffed. Jesus painfully understands that human kinship cannot be allowed to affect the pattern of his ministry. Jesus is not rebuking or denying his family but he is denying the role which they would impose upon him. Jesus wants his mother and his brothers to understand that his actions at Cana or Jerusalem will depend upon his volition and not their persistence.

The scene at the cross also has been considered an inappropriate action on the part of Jesus. There are those who say that the brothers will have the legal responsibility for their mother and, even if Jesus is the eldest, he has no right to place his mother in the hands of the beloved disciple. The story is further challenged by the fact that later Mary shows up in the company of the brothers in the book of Acts.

What is crucial to accepting this adoption scene at Golgotha is the realization that Jesus hangs on the cross to satisfy the spiritual needs of all, including his mother. This point is intensified by his charge to the disciple to oversee the spiritual welfare of his mother. Certainly there are others who will care for this woman as to her legal or physical needs. But, since the family has not yet been won to an understanding of his messiahship, they cannot fulfill this major responsibility which Jesus has for his mother. The beloved disciple must take the place of Jesus as spiritual tutor until such a time arrives that the family is one in the spirit with their elder brother.

In Plutarch's *Lives* there is a story that is almost an exact opposite of the story of Jesus. Caius Marcius Coriolanus was a great Roman warrior who fell out of favor with the people of Rome. As the story develops, he eventually laid seige to Rome as leader of an enemy army. It appeared that he would be victorious over his former home city until his mother and his wife appeared before him. His mother cried out that he would never be victorious unless he first trampled "upon the corpse of her that brought you into life." She then called for him to perform a deed loftier than destroying Rome or betraying the army which followed him: she called for him to create peace and friendship on both sides.

Caius Marcius then exclaimed: "O mother! what is this you have done to me! . . . You have gained a victory, fortunate enough for the Romans, but destructive to your son; whom you, though no one else, have defeated." The truth of this was seen when soon afterwards he was murdered during a public debate over his actions at the gate to Rome.

Caius Marcius was a rash fighter. He was vindictive. But he allowed his mother to turn him aside from his base pursuits with the result that he perished while her more lofty goals were achieved.

Jesus Christ was a purposeful man who pursued peace and redemption. He did not allow his family to turn him aside from his glorious pursuits. (Though I do not intend by the contrast to say that his family urged upon him base actions, merely actions of lower value.) He too died, but did not perish; rather he has accomplished the redemption which was his goal.

From the interaction with his family we may conclude that the closest scrutiny of Jesus will not reflect any character defects. They knew him to be a good man. But this testimony is incomplete. The testimony of faith says that he is Savior. Neither human kinship, argument, nor miracle can do the work of faith.

What Are You Made Of?

Who is it, Lord?   John 13:25

Boys are made of snips and snails and puppy dog tails. Girls are made of sugar and spice and everything nice. But what are you? The psalmist ponders that. "What is man that you think of him?"

Sidney Cave has entitled a book *The Christian Estimate of Man*. I find that title instructive in its humility. Rather than be dogmatic about inherent human nature, let's observe for a little while and make an estimate about humanity. Read John 13:21-30 and we will use it as a laboratory.

> After Jesus said this, he was deeply troubled, and declared openly: "I tell you the truth, one of you is going to betray me." The disciples looked at one another, completely puzzled about whom he meant. One of the disciples, whom Jesus loved, was sitting next to Jesus. Simon Peter motioned to him and said, "Ask him who it is that he is talking about." So that disciple moved closer to Jesus' side and asked, "Who is it, Lord?" Jesus answered, "I will dip the bread in the sauce and give it to him; he is the man." So he took a piece of bread, dipped it, and gave it to Judas, the son of Simon Iscariot.

> As soon as Judas took the bread, Satan went into him.
> Jesus said to him, "Hurry and do what you must!"
> (None of those at the table understood what Jesus said
> to him. Since Judas was in charge of the money bag,
> some of the disciples thought that Jesus had told him to
> go to buy what they needed for the feast, or else that he
> had told him to give something to the poor.) Judas accepted the bread and went out at once. It was night.

What can we learn about humanity? What can we learn about ourselves? *Our reaction to Judas indicates something decent about ourselves.* I am not talking about a holier-than-thou attitude. I do not mean to say that we are proud because of a self-confidence that we would never deny our Lord. Peter's experience of denying his Lord halts this kind of thinking. Rather, I observe a good, healthy sensitivity to the diabolical betrayal of Jesus Christ.

Here is our working hypothesis for the next few paragraphs: Being human is good. James Sellers points out that the Reformation principle of *sola fide* (faith alone) is often overstated. In the traditional development of that doctrine man is described as throughly bankrupt morally and spiritually. Well, yes, a person without Christ does have problems, but that individual is not an empty void. The natural person has some values.

You can see the strong values of humanity at many points. All artistic attempts do not end in pornography. People are capable of producing beautiful representations of life, beautiful objects, beautiful motions. All scientific attempts are not aimed at displacing religion. People are capable of making the activities of life more comfortable, more efficient, more effective. All political endeavors are not exploitations of the common man. People are capable of organizing themselves in such a way as to secure greater good for a greater number of people.

The art gallery downtown; the drama at the college; every

What Are You Made Of?

modern convenience in your home, plus the lighting, heat, and air conditioning at church; human relations councils and some of the efforts of good men in political offices—all of these indicate the potential for good in humanity.

There is a responsiveness within us that knows the difference between betrayal and fidelity. At times this responsiveness issues in expedient, political good; at times it brings forth benevolent, social, or personal good; at times it produces spiritual, moral good.

Can we make a generalization? Do we have enough collective experience between writer and reader to say that our observation substantiates the hypothesis? Everywhere we find humanity, we find a struggle to better the person, the society, the environment.

I can call in some heavy support for the research: God created man and when he finished his creation he pronounced it good—and it still is.

Preacher Blumhardt is often quoted as saying, "Man requires two conversions." One conversion is from the natural life to the spiritual life. And then, to avoid asceticism, one conversion is from the spiritual life to the natural.

Now here is something that we must learn: it is a good thing to be a human being. You are not a worm. You are not the lowest of creation but the highest. And this is a good biblical teaching.

But there is more data observed within our laboratory. We react to Jesus along with the disciples and *our reaction to Jesus indicates something amiss about ourselves.* This is our second working hypothesis: there is something wrong with humanity.

You say you don't believe in original sin. You oppose that determinism that says you are going to sin and you are guilty. "How can I be guilty when I didn't have a choice," you argue. You oppose the preaching that beats you over the head with Adam's sin and attempts to make you feel like dirt. You rebel at thinking which says in effect that God put us in a confined maze so that we have no choice but come out where it says SIN because that is the only exit. And it disgusts you to hear of a God who gleefully pronounces us all guilty and sings choruses while preparing a cauldron of hell.

Well, all right, let's ditch original sin. But while we are looking for a new theology, what about the laboratory data of rapid pulses, involuntary gasps, tightened throats, and nervous twitches that accompanies everyone's, "Is it I?" Yes, there is a lot of muddled thinking about how sin got here. But it is here. Every disciple had to face up to the fact that it could have been himself of whom the Lord spoke. And you know it would be your response, also. Maybe we ought to keep "original sin" as a doctrine but patch it up some.

"Of course," you say, "we all make mistakes and they embarrass us, too; but embarrassment is not guilt. And after all, even Judas wasn't all that bad." Is Judas at fault? Some seem to think he was simply trying to control his circumstances. Now, if that is the case, that is quite laudable. Maybe Judas was just attempting to force a showdown. Maybe Judas was just trying to bring together all the epochal factors that would expose the Messiah to his task and thus usher in the kingdom of God. Maybe his so-called betrayal was really a grand gesture to initiate Utopia. Well, now, no one wants to condemn a herculean effort.

But is that really the case? The Gospels describe Judas as a penny-ante sneak thief. When Mary spills costly ointment on the feet of her Savior scant hours before his death, Judas objects that the money could have been used for the poor. But John makes us privy to his insight when he tells us that Judas really only wants the money in the treasury where he can pilfer it. Claiming concern for the indigent, he actually cares for himself alone. Piqued by Jesus' rebuff he stomps off to the Sanhedrin in spite. A petty little man, he acts as a rash, tempermental brat. The religious leaders who wanted

Christ's head were eager to find a means to get him without stirring the mob. Judas allows himself to be used and without thinking through the outcome of his actions he singles out Jesus for the apprehensive police with a big show of affection.

Later Judas realizes that events were in control of him instead of the other way around. Again thinking childishly he believes the simple statement, "He is innocent," will stop the machine that he has helped to set in motion. He feels that giving back the money will remove his guilt. He almost drowns in the awesomeness of the priest's retort, "That's your problem, isn't it?"

Judas throws the money on the floor of the holy place in the Temple. (Had the priests gone there to get away from the pest? Or had Judas barged in where he didn't belong?) What irony that the money is thrown in that area that speaks of atonement.

The details of his suicide are not particularly clear. Well, who would know anything specific about it except Judas? Evidently, he hanged himself and there is something about a neglected body that . . . ah well, maybe the whole thing is an uglier story than we care to admit or to hear about.

John says Judas went out into the night. John always does more than state the simple facts. His style indicates the darkness of that life.

You know, as you look at the progress of mankind you find that with our ability to create heaven we continually drag hell along with us. Carl Henry reminds us that the nadir of human moral bankruptcy is found in Hitler's Germany in our century. And the point is not that Germans are the worst people of humanity, nor that the twentiety century is the worst time of all history, nor even that Hitler was the embodiment of evil. The point is that humanity is always found sinful.

Hitler was guilty, Judas was guilty, Adam was guilty, but they aren't the only ones. Maybe it is time for a tentative generalization. Our hypothesis appears to be correct. Everywhere we find man we find a struggle with that which would make us, and our neighbors, and our world worse.

How many times is this realization reported? David—a man after God's own heart—sobbed out his confession of sin.

Ezra was prostrate because of the sin of his people. Nehemiah confessed his sin and that of his father's house. Isaiah: "Woe is me." Job: "I have sinned."

Jeremiah quotes God as saying, "Lye soap cannot wash off the marks of iniquity." Recall Anselm's most quoted sentence, "You have not yet considered what a heavy weight sin is." Ah, here is the problem—we discover a Judas within each of us. Not just an ignorance that doesn't know what Jesus really wants of us; not just a clumsiness that bungles the situation; but a determination to rebel against the Lord. A determination to spitefully say to God, like the child, "I'm going to hurt you."

Haven't you acted out Adam's story? Here is the tree of experiencing the difference between good and evil. The day you taste of it is the day of awareness of that within you that calls for death. The point of the Genesis story is not that you are created a sinner, not that sin is in your blood. The point is that you are responsible for your actions. The fault, dear Brutus, is not in our stars—nor our genealogy—but in ourselves.

If we can trust our observation, we have found man sinful. But if we suddenly awake to our lot in desperation as did Judas, then we are liable to desperately miss the whole point, as did Judas. Jesus did not come to condemn us. Our desperation, it seems, has done this already.

Jesus Christ is the Good Man. Jesus Christ is the source of mankind's realization of the good potential. Jesus Christ can reconcile the you that is somehow wrong with the you who holds the hope of goodness.

What is your nature? You are human. That is an openended thing to say. You are still becoming. Humanity is not

What Are You Made Of?

yet a finished product. We can say that a human is not the devil. No human person shall ever be the devil. This may or may not say something about hell. It certainly says something about earth. It says that humanity is not the full embodiment of evil; humanity is not a worm; humanity is not trash. We can say, also, that no man or woman is God and never shall be. This may or may not say something about heaven. It certainly says something about earth. It says humanity is not the final authority; humanity is not completely self-sufficient; humanity is not all-wise. People are people. Humanity is more than animal, less than angel. If we think ourselves devils, we degrade mankind in a false pietism. If we think ourselves gods, then we betray our Lord.

Whatever you are, you will only reach your potential by loyalty to Jesus, not by betrayal.

Rude Arrogance

It is better for you to have one man die for the people, instead of the whole nation being destroyed.
John 11:50

There is double and triple irony in the statement of Caiaphas to the council. He had been able to suggest a course of action which would vindicate his loyalty to the Roman authority, display his concern for his fellow countrymen, and gratify his hatred. He had, in one sentence voiced his selfish and political expediency while uttering profound, divine truth.

His pronouncement begins roughly, "You do not know a thing!" This man is arrogant and rude. Josephus charged that the Sadducees were boorish and rude even among themselves. Whether or not the fact that Josephus was a Pharisee influenced his opinion of the Sadducees, I cannot determine. But Caiaphas seems to establish the validity of Josephus' opinion.

The Evangelist inserts his opinion that Caiaphas was prophesying the atonement because he was high priest *that* year. This rudely arrogant man was sensitive to the moment with all its dangers but he was not sensitive to *the* moment in history. He, the high priest of the chosen people of God, did not know that the "one man" of whom he spoke would become the focus of attention for humanity in *that* year.

Caiaphas was a powerful man. He stood at a critical midpoint between the people of the land, the Jews, and their conquerors, the Romans. As sometimes happens with those who have power, Caiaphas was dangerously, rudely arrogant.

The rudely arrogant are dangerous on a large scale. Greed for power knows no bounds. The more power one senses within his grasp, the hungrier he is for greater power. As I have said, Caiaphas was in a position of considerable power and responsibility. As long as there were no civil disturbances to upset the Roman governor, the high priest and those about him held virtual control of Jerusalem.

It was an expedient arrangement. The priests raked in a fair revenue from the Temple and its allied business interests. The Romans kept control of the situation without showing armor or rattling sabers. The trade-off remained quite placid but could be upset by any of the motley parade of messiahs which might come out of the woodwork. Oh, Jesus wasn't the only one. Ever so often a liberator would appear and there was always the possibility that one of them would so set off the masses that Roman power would be unleashed to the destruction of the nation and the collaborators' playhouse.

Caiaphas understood Machiavelli long before *The Prince* was penned. Machiavelli affirmed that it was not necessary for the prince to be merciful, faithful, humane, upright, or religious; but it was vitally essential that he appear to have those qualities. "Everyone sees what you appear to be," counseled the Italian political philosopher, "few really know what you are, and those few dare not oppose themselves to the opinion of the many." It would appear that the high priest was a political functionary at one of the lower levels. But that is not to minimize the danger he presents to his nation should he allow or cause some set of circumstances which would fire up the dreaded war machine of the Roman army.

Indeed, he arrogantly places his nation on a course that proves expensive on the largest scale. During the Jewish-Roman war of the seventh decade of *that* century Jerusalem was under seige by Titus. Many nationalists (One might call such confident nationalism arrogance.) were so confident in their cause that they filled Jerusalem at a time of seige with masses of pilgrims come to observe the Passover. What they accomplished was the tragic loss of the nation.

Which brings up another point: *The rudely arrogant are dangerous to the innocent.* Unfortunately, expediency is the only standard for arrogant politicians. I must make it clear that there is a kind of arrogancy which has not learned the value of a judicious flexibility. But that is not Caiaphas' problem. He is overly flexible. For such unprincipled expediency nothing is sacred. Herodotus recounts the lecturing of Darius on the subject.

> An untruth must be spoken, where need requires. For whether men lie, or say true, it is with one and the same object. Men lie, because they think to gain by deceiving others; and speak the truth, because they expect to get something by their true speaking, and to be trusted afterwards in more important matters.

Therefore, the only principle is personal gain, the only guidance toward such gain is expediency. When the ground rules consist of such an absence of rules, the naive, the innocent, the idealistic optimist, and the starry-eyed dreamer are all easy prey. Machiavelli advised that the prince learn the craft of expediency, or "how to disguise," realizing that "men are so simple, and so subject to present necessities, that he who seeks to deceive will always find someone who will allow himself to be deceived." In the words of a later Machiavelli, "There's a sucker born every minute."

Jesus was neither naive nor starry-eyed, but he was innocent and did stand in the place of all of us gullible marks who fair so poorly with the con artists of the world. His innocence nowhere enters into the calculations of Caiaphas. It was expedient for one to die. Innocence is beside the point. Retention of his place of power and manipulation matters more than the innocence or personality of the man before him.

Expediency in the sense of unprincipledness is dangerous. It is immoral but the immorality is well disguised. Actually Caiaphas proclaims his wisdom in the form of a moral choice which would require one to select the obvious "proper righteous outcome." An artificial choice is offered: either take the simple alternative of the loss of one obscure life or the extreme devastation of the nation. The balances are incorrectly weighted in favor of the second choice. Should he have offered with the first alternative the term assassination and the subsequent shriveling of soul which attaches to such expedient choices, the term "loss of nation" might have been shifted to the other side. Ah! but the false choices which consider no third or fourth alternatives and wear the cloak of "oughtness" about them here, as with regularity elsewhere, suck in the gullible.

In a lively debate Samuel Johnson prodded the playwright Goldsmith about his motives of pleasing the king. Goldsmith rejoined, "I *do* wish to please him. I remember a line in Dreyden 'And every poet is the monarch's friend.' It ought to be reversed." Goldsmith would have it read, "And the monarch is every poet's friend." Johnson replied that Dreyden had a better line which made the same point and quoted:

    For colleges on bounteous Kings depend,
    And never rebel was to arts a friend.

But Johnson and Goldsmith limit the options severely. Perhaps and established government is more likely to be a patron of the arts, but the disestablished frequently provide art with its soul. Institutions frequently provide the grants that enable researchers to tackle the injustices of life; but institutions just as frequently grind up the little people in the unjust cogs which expediency requires to be turned. The choice of either/or is sometimes artificially simple and for that reason can be improper or even immoral.

Caiaphas calls for assassination but not in so harsh an expression. His abstract statment masks the ugliness of his proposal. One can almost picture him on stage in Shakespear's *King Henry VI* nodding approval to Cardinal Beaufort's judgment on the Duke of Gloucester:

That he should die is worthy policy;

But yet we want a colour for his death:

'This meet he be condemn'd by course of law.

Matching the danger they represent in so many other directions it is true that *the rudely arrogant are dangerous to themselves.* Theirs is a way of life which is isolated and self-centered. If Caiaphas is preeminently important and everyone else and all circumstances are his tools, then he has no protection from some offended subject who might turn on him. Or, he has protection only as long as his expedience works, only as long as he can manipulate others to protect him. In a few short years the system did him in. Vitellius, proconsul of Syria removed Pilate from office in A.D. 36 and with Pilate went Caiaphas.

It is obvious that Caiaphas had no one to stand with him on his level back-to-back. He had no comrade, no shared trusts, none who could be Thou to his I. The platform of arrogancy is lofty, but it is narrow and lonely and and tends to cause acrophobia just as it reveals itself as gallows with opening trapdoor. As he manipulated others with his policy of expediency, so is he removed from the board: a pawn to be surrendered in the expedient pursuit of other goals.

His story reechoes through other lives. Leo Tolstoy knew Caiaphas. Witness the shadow of the high priest in *War and Peace:*

"The execution of the Duc d'Enghien," declared Monsieur Pierre, "was a political necessity, and it seems to me that Napoleon showed greatness of soul by not fearing to take on himself the whole responsibility of that deed."

"Dieu! Mon Dieu!" muttered Anna Pavlovna in a

terrified whisper.

"What, Monsieur Pierre . . . Do you consider that assassination shows greatness of soul?" said the little princess, smiling and drawing her work nearer to her . . her . . . .

"I say so . . . Napoleon . . . could not stop short for the sake of one man's life."

Of course not! Neither could Caiaphas nor Pilate. It is expedient that one man not block progress. But let's see now. Things have gotten a little confused. What is it that is at stake in the death of one man?

What Is Truth?

"I was born and came into the world for this one purpose, to speak about the truth. Whoever belongs to the truth listens to me."

"And what is truth?" Pilate asked.

John 18:37-38

Dusk and dawn are confusing. This is the story of that day when dawn met dusk and left a whole day of confusion. There is an amazing quality about those hours between day and night and again between night and day that makes everything seem a bit unreal. It is no less true here as we see the Sanhedrin together before dawn holding two illegal trials. Surely it cannot be true, but it is. They meet at night, an illegal act. They condemn this man to death on the same day of his trial, another illegality. Now he is brought to Pilate in order to receive the death sentence which they do not have the power to give.

The crowd will not enter the judgment hall on the grounds that it would cause ceremonial pollution. What quibbling over a small thing when they are about to commit the most heinous crime known to mankind.

Pilate begins to hold trial outside which was not unusual for the Romans. They always made their trials as public as possible. However, the Sanhedrin does not want a trial. A trial would expose their flimsy charges. They call for a sentence. They come with a good-sized show in order to carry the argument with the force of display rather than the force of logic. The high priest is here as well as a large crowd. They clamor and raise a commotion, but Pilate is not carried away by the mob. He senses the attempts to sway his decision and responds, "If this man is so bad, you try him." After all, you see, anyone as bad as this display indicates would be quickly found guilty by any court.

It hurts their pride to admit that there are some things that Rome will not permit them to do. The people are forced to respond, "No, we cannot render the death verdict." Luke tells us that they then charge Jesus with claiming kingship. At this point Pilate takes Jesus inside and thus gets away from the crowd and, for a time, makes Jesus his prisoner so that he can handle him as he sees fit.

It is hard to believe that the mob is serious about the charge. Pilate looks at Jesus and asks, *"You,* are *you* a king?" Even as he says it, Pilate realizes this must be a foolish question. How can Jesus answer that question? He has been charged with claiming a political kingship, something he had many times denied. If he answers yes, he will admit more than the truth. If he answers no, he will deny more than the lie. Yes, he is a king. No, he is not the kind of king that the mob or Pilate would believe.

The only recourse is for Jesus to answer the question with a question. "Are you personally seeking answer, or are you merely repeating the accusations of the Sanhedrin?" But Pilate has no personal interest. He is not religious and does not care about the common man's foolish ideas concerning this harmless looking, ragged prisoner.

Jesus attempts to tell Pilate exactly what sort of king he is. Three times he explains to Pilate, "The kingship that is mine . . ." to indicate that he is a different kind of king than the world has ever known. Pilate's response is contemptuous, "What sort of king are *you?*"

"You say, 'I am a king.' For this I was born and for this I

What Is Truth?

came into the world, so that I might witness to the truth; all who are of the truth hear my voice." As Pilate hears the word "truth," he perhaps thinks of these Israelites who hate the Roman empire but somehow have become exceptionally patriotic. He perhaps is aware of their finicky reluctance to enter the place of a Gentile while showing utter disregard at seeking an innocent man's life. He perhaps is aware of how unjust the hall of justice can become. As he shrugs his shoulders and goes back outside, he mutters, *"What is truth?"*

Man's basic search is a search for truth. Notice the question is not what is *the* truth. The question asks whether such a thing exists. What is *truth?* Truth is that which is right. It is that which is stable. It is the foundation of life. Truth is that dependable solidness that gives us a proper perspective. Truth is that which I should do, I should think, I should believe. Truth is the opposite of everything that is false, unreal, or artificial.

But we still have the question, "What is truth?" This question is voiced everytime you ask yourself: "What is right? What is necessary? What is good? What is to be gained?" Anytime the lazy, malcontent sponger asks himself "How much do I have to do to get by?" he is basically asking, "What is truth?" In other words we are asking the question of the basic values of life. What is meaningful?

"What is truth?" In a major city a man watches some of the Christian leaders of our nation attempt to express a protest against hate and prejudice; and he watches some of the courageous, purposeful followers who march shoulder to shoulder with troublemakers, dirty "longhairs," and people who just want to start a fight. The sight of such an incongruous mixture stirs the question, "What is truth?"

In Washington, in Southeast Asia, in dark corners or on bright streets, anywhere in the world you might come upon this question. In a state capitol there was a hearing on gambling before a committee of the state representatives. The pro-gambling group had a minister appear for their side. He told the committee that the Bible does not teach that men are to live like angels. He expressed the conviction that men are naturally sinful and they ought to accept the fact and enjoy it. "What is truth?"

This searching, this seeking, this quest for truth is a desire of humanity for conviction. It is a desire to really know in the heart that anything is right. You want to believe in something so strongly that you can live for that cause or die for it and know that you are doing the right thing. Oh, if a man could stand before a cross with conviction and risk everything knowing that even if he loses it all, it is right and good! But there always seems to be a hesitancy. Maybe we can understand a little better what Jesus meant when he said, "the truth shall make you free." If you are doing the right thing and know it, you have a certain freedom, a carefree attitude that gives a freshness and vigor to your actions.

"Pilate, what are you going to do with the prisoner?"

"I must interrogate him and discover whether the charges are just or unjust."

"The prisoner speaks of the standard of truth. How will you deal with him?"

"Truth? What is truth? It is too early—or too late—to think of such terms."

Pilate asks the right question of the right person, but fails to wait for an answer. And he needs that answer desperately. Pilate goes back and forth between the crowd and Jesus in fear. The crowd speaks of a claim that Jesus is the Son of God. This frightens Pilate. Jesus has a greater sense of confidence and authority than Pilate. This frightens the Governor. The crowd threatens reprisals from Rome. This frightens him. Pilate has already tried to free Jesus by offering Barabbas to the bloodthirsty mob, but that did not work, Finally, he lets the crowd make the decision for him. He hands

Later there is a complaint concerning the wording on the sign placed on Jesus' cross. Pilate firmly asserts his authority, "What I have written stays written." Bravo! our little hero. Don't you wish you had been as firm earlier? But how can a man know when to be firm and how to decide? Yes, Pilate needed an answer to his question, What is truth?

God's basic character is truth. Jesus revealed God as truth. If Pilate had waited, he might have heard Jesus say as he had said before, "I am the truth!" Jesus reveals to us that God is essentially truth. He is that which is real, certain, stable, constant, meaningful. He does not say that what God says is truth, though we would understand that to be the case. He says, "I am the truth." Discovering truth in personality rather than proposition frees us from having to have all the answers. We know, instead, the Person.

There is a recurring theme throughout the Bible that God is a rock. He is often addressed as the "Rock of my salvation." This meaningful picture shows God as a foundation stone. This is one way of saying that God is truth.

Anytime that you want to measure something, whether it is surveying property or weighing potatoes, you have to have a scale, a norm by which you measure. It may be feet, pounds, or hours; but there is a standard. Jesus Christ is our standard. He gives us perspective by which to measure life. He is truth.

Jesus' task is shaped by God's character. Because God is truth, Jesus did what was right. If Pilate had only paid attention to what Jesus did say to him, he would have been helped. Jesus told him that it was his job to witness to the truth. This was the task that Jesus came to accomplish: to answer the question, "What is truth?" It was his mission to point men to the rock of salvation. It was his task to be the truth, to be the standard of life. This is what Jesus was doing at that very moment. living out the messianic task of being the truth.

Notice that his task was to be truth, not to protect truth. Some try to protect truth by crucifixion, some by vote to censure or by administrative removal from office, some by a laugh of ridicule. The defenders of truth sometimes become its worst enemies. Truth does not need to be protected so much as it needs simply to be shared.

The essential character of truth—the standard that Jesus was and is—this is a stabilizing factor for his followers. If Pilate had but listened, he would have heard Jesus as he said, "All who are of the truth hear my voice."

For that person who desires to know the truth, there is a voice that gives directions. There is a standard of truth, and it is not one that is hidden in some musty law book. The Christian can but listen and hear that Christ speaks. It is such a comfort to know that truth is accessible to all who know him who is the truth. It is not so much any one thing he says that guides us, but it is the fact that his voice serves as an audible lighthouse directing us toward him. What is the right thing to do, to think, to believe? Portray the actions of the truth and you have your answer.

We must quarrel with Pilate about his grammar. He asked, "*What* is truth?" He uses the neuter which is the wrong gender. Truth is not a moral philosophy. It is not a legal system. Truth is Jesus Christ! We correct Pilate's "*What* is truth?" with the answer "*He* is the truth!"

Beyond Skepticism

"Stop your doubting and believe!" Thomas answered him, "My Lord and my God!"
John 20:27-28

Life is full of surprises. Perhaps the biggest surprises are found in people. Too often we pigeon-hole a person, we place someone in a stereotype and think of him one-dimensionally; then, when we discover some new trait in that person, we are surprised. This is particularly true in our country because of our short-story mentality.

We tend to think of people and events in terms of the short stories we read. In a short story a personality is never adequately developed. The author must present one facet of a personality; there is not space for more than that. Because we are fans of the short story and the condensed novel, we tend to see those about us in a short-story frame of reference.

Thomas is victim of that sort of thought. Thomas has been called a doubter, but this is a caricature of the man. It is an emphasis of one feature of his personality. We find a larger description in three scattered verses in the book of John.

When Jesus speaks of returning to the Jerusalem suburb where his friend Lazarus has died, Thomas says to the disciples, "Let us go along with the Teacher, that we may die together with him."

Later, while Thomas is confused by the reality that they have, after all, not died, he hears Jesus speaking of his death in veiled terms. Jesus tells his disciples he is leaving them but they know where he is going. Thomas replies, "Lord, we do not know where you are going; how can we know the way to get there?"

Finally, Thomas has suffered the loss of his leader, and to the pain of grief has been added the confusion of hearing the other disciples claim that Jesus is not dead. Incredibly they insist they have seen the Lord. To which Thomas retorts, "If I do not see the scars of the nails in his hands, and put my finger where the nails were, and my hand in his side, I will not believe."

Thomas is often castigated and occasionally lauded as a doubter. But this is a very limited vision of the man. Consider these characteristics as descriptive of Thomas:

He was loyal. In fact he has been called valiantly loyal. This is what we see in the first episode. He knows without any doubt that a return to the Jerusalem area will bring death; but if that is what Jesus wants, that is where Thomas will follow. Now, of course, you realize that the time comes when Jesus does die and all the disciples ran, which must include Thomas. But this does not do away with the fact that Thomas was willing to go to Jerusalem. At that time his action showed a deep strain of loyalty.

Thomas must have related to the person Jesus more than to any cause or principle. This is loyalty, an unusual quality. Have you considered how often we sacrifice people to points to be made?

He was courageous. This is the backbone of his loyalty. Thomas faces the ominous future quite openly and says, "It is a disastrous route but I will take it." That is what courage is: to acknowledge danger and still remain loyal to commitments.

Out of World War I comes a story about an artillery officer.

His duty was to go up in a captive balloon, mark where the shells from the guns fell, and indicate to the gunners whether the shells fell short or went over the target. It was a most dangerous assignment. Because the balloon was held stationary there was no means of dodging. He was a sitting target for the guns and the planes of the enemy. A friend said of this officer, "Every time he went up in that balloon he was sick with nerves, but he wouldn't quit."

That is what courage is: courage is not doing something brave without feeling any fear at all. If you do not feel any fear, you haven't done anything courageous. Courage is when you sense all the danger involved and you do something anyway. And this is what Thomas illustrates.

He was honest. Thomas is criticized for his doubts but this too often ignores his uncompromising honesty. Here was a man who wanted solid facts, who evidently had little poetry in his soul. He was far too honest and far too much in earnest to be satisfied with any vague and pious expressions. Jesus says to his disciples that they know the way; and Thomas responds with remarkable candor: "No, we don't. You may think we know, but we do not." He actually contradicts Jesus as he says, "It is all dark and blank to me."

When the disciples confront him with their testimony and call for an acceptance of it by Thomas, he simply tells them that he cannot say he believes when he does not believe. How refreshingly honest!

He was able to change. Now this is not one of the weightier points about Thomas. He could not accept the resurrection until Jesus appeared before him. Then, when the facts were presented to him, as one commentator puts it, he was able to change his opinion. Well, in that circumstance, who wouldn't? But when you consider the monumental stubbornness that is loose in some parts of this world, perhaps it is worthy of mentioning that the ability to change one's mind is a virtue to be cultivated.

These four characteristics have been framed positively. Let me state a negative characteristic of the man Thomas. John Claypool sees it as a weakness that *he was pessimistic.* Thomas always expected the worst. "We will go to Jerusalem," he laments to the other disciples, "but we will die." To his Lord he complains, "You can tell us about what you are doing, but we will not understand." "You may think you have seen the Lord," Thomas pouts, "but it could never happen." Claypool sees pessism as the chief mark in Thomas' life. And he says of this attitude that it is presumptuous since Thomas cannot know either the ups or downs of the future. Pessimism is also heretical; it is a faithless attitude. In contrast, Claypool contends, "We should be open to the future and hopeful."

I believe this is a valid conclusion regarding Thomas, as well as a helpful insight on life. It was perhaps because of his feeling of pessimistic hopelessness that he missed the visit of the resurrected Lord to the gathering of the disciples. If that is true, then his pessimism allowed Thomas to consign himself to an extra week of misery.

So I have described Thomas as loyal, courageous, honest, able to change, but pessimistic. If this is a fair characterization of Thomas, what lessons do we learn by looking at his life? Let me zero in on his honesty and his pessimism. These traits combine to make Thomas a skeptic.

There is a qualitative difference between skepticism and doubt. We are talking about a deeper, more far-reaching characteristic of man by saying he is a skeptic rather than a doubter. Even if you talk about his loyalty and courage, you describe characteristics that can intensify skepticism.

I see three lessons in Thomas' skepticism.

1. The life of pessimistic Thomas shows us that there is room for such troubled, questing minds in the company of Jesus. These are the peace disturbers, the unkosher bunch. Sometimes we have a tendency to call this person disloyal because his skepticism attacks the established order. But this is

not necessarily the case as Thomas so well shows.

We had better be willing to make room for such a person because he could be any one of us. Thomas a Kempis says in his *Imitation of Christ* that he never knew anyone so religious that he had not had sometimes a withdrawing of grace, a decrease of zeal. Then he confesses his grief that sometimes he came to his worship responsibility with "such lukewarmness yea coldness. I grieve to think that I remain so dry, without affection of heart."

2. We had better be willing to make room for these people because they may be the more creative among us. Either from their own tormented souls or by virtue of the stirring of their skepticism, these agitated hearts become a catalyst for creative moments. This honest, courageous skeptic makes Jesus answer real questions and perhaps, as a result, Jesus gives us his best answers. What are his answers to Thomas? First, he takes them to a grave where he calls Lazarus back to life. Second, he makes that remarkable statement: "I am the way, the truth, and the life; no man comes to the Father except by me." And then, third, when Thomas' hesitation causes him to make that gross demand of resurrection evidence, the answer was an appearance of our Lord to the skeptic.

Don't you see the weight of this evidence? They were not all a gullible bunch easily hyptonized or mystified. One man was extremely skeptical; yet he was convinced. The skeptic was convinced and the appearance has strong apologetical value. After all, if Thomas believed, how can anyone doubt?

You see the value of having someone around asking very hard questions. Here was one radically honest, courageous enough to face tradition and say, "I do not believe that is necessarily the case." When there is someone like that in the group, you are going to have to hear the best kind of answers. Sham cannot stand before this sort of probing.

Here is a great service: ask the questions which say: "This is where I hurt! Here is what is really bugging me." The church needs those questions. Questions have played a valuable role in growth. It is extremely important to a developing heritage to allow conversation and questioning. So often there is a lack of communication, there are various shadows on words spoken that camouflage meaning, and we need someone to say, "I just do not understand what you are saying," or, "I cannot believe that. I need stronger evidence."

Halford Luccock quotes a pastor who claims that most people join a church on "confusion of faith." If this is so, it may be because people have not been allowed to express their doubts, confusions, or skepticism. Too many church members have not cared about asking questions. They have not cared about probing and poking. Perhaps theirs is a spoon-fed religion where they never worried whether they understood what was funneled into their systems or not. If there is one characteristic consistently true of the average church member, it may be his confusion.

Even if you have never been confused, you can profit by that other person's question and resulting answer. I don't mean to say that anyone has all the answers. But even if answers are not to be found, we are much better off groping with real questions.

3. There is a final lesson to be learned from the life of Thomas. Thomas is an example of the proper outcome of skepticism: he leaves skepticism for solid faith. When Jesus presents himself to Thomas, the response of this loyal disciple who was able to change is, "My Lord and my God!"

Skepticism may be worth a visit, but it is no place to live. If you have honest doubts or pessimistic forbodings, pursue your skepticism until it leads you to faith. Skepticism should be a tool, however, and not a life-style. It should always be adjectival or adverbial; never let it become an appositive noun. I mean by that, let someone say of you, "He responded skeptically," but not, "He is a skeptic." Whatever values skepticism may have for us, in the last analysis I agree with John Claypool, the Christian life should be marked by an open, hopeful attitude. The proper outcome of the probing of skepticism is to say, "My Lord and my God!"

As a concluding note, let me remind you of the entry lines of Jesus both times that he appeared among the assembled disciples. He said when Thomas was absent and when he was present:

"Peace be to you!"

Those must have been happy words for skeptical Thomas to have heard.

Searching for Death; Finding Life

Mary!... Do not hold on to me. John 20:16,17

Christmas morning when our three-year-old finally found her sleepy-eyed way to the presents under the tree she had not quite rejoined our world. Upon opening one package she exclaimed, "Oh, it's just what I wanted, a hockey game!" I corrected her, "Honey, that isn't a hockey game. It's a turtle." "Oh how nice!" she decided, "a hockey turtle." For some reason we are all made that way. When the mind gets started in one direction, the momentum keeps the train of thought going even if the direction is 180 degrees wrong.

While it is true that any one of us might have a hard time doing an about face when we are wrong; the rest of us, those looking on, can usually learn something through the misunderstanding. The misunderstanding which leads others to understanding is a popular theme. As you read the *Dialogues* of Plato you discover that Socrates built his reputation for wisdom on the principle of understanding through misunderstanding. By pursuing through question and answer countless roads to error, he usually came to the truth. Vaudeville has made the device a slap-stick necessity. In its simplest form one hears the straightman repeat for emphasis the straight line, over-acting his puzzlement, to heighten anticipation of the punch line.

Understanding through misunderstanding is also a device of the Fourth Gospel. Oscar Cullmann underlines this tendency of the disciples toward misunderstanding. They appear quite mystified by all that goes on during the life of Jesus; but receive understanding according to Jesus' own prophecy after his death when the promised Spirit directs them "into the truth."

In the case of Mary Magdalene you have the supreme example of John's theme of understanding through misunderstanding. Here it is not a case of Philip misunderstanding what Jesus says about himself and the Father, this is not a matter of confused concepts; rather, Mary has confused personalities. She misunderstands the living Jesus himself rather than his teaching. How frustrating and confusing it must have been for her, but how instructive and inspiring it is for those of us who watch.

Hers was a desperate search. It is reminiscent of Song of Solomon 3:1-4.

> One night my lover was missing from my bed. I got up to look for him but couldn't find him. I went out into the streets of the city and the roads to seek him, but I searched in vain. The police stopped me and I said to them, 'Have you seen him anywhere, this one I love so much?' It was only a little while afterwards that I found him and held him and would not let him go until I had brought him into my childhood home, into my mother's old bedroom. (The Children's Living Bible)

Mary is equally desperate. She is so disturbed that she is not impressed by the presence of angels nor does she recognize him who is the object of her search. Martin Luther was amazed by her state of mind. "No man is so bravehearted but what he would be terrified if unexpectedly he should behold an angel; and she even a woman. Yet she moves about

Searching for Death, Finding Life

so that she neither sees nor hears nor inquires about anything; so completely her heart is elsewhere."

It is not hard to see in her desperation our modern flight from death. Modern prophets at every opportunity have chastened us for making death obscene for our society as sex was obscene for the Victorians. We are offended should someone pronounce us mortal—perishable. The language of denial, the funeral charades which violently push the real event out of sight, the sophisticated dogma that mature man is only interested in this life and not "pie-in-the-sky" these are all steps in the frantically choreographed "Dance of the Magdalene." With her we are in a frenzy to find some proof that it doesn't really happen. Surely his body is here somewhere. If I look hard enough, I will find him and all will return to the way it was.

She is looking for Jesus as he was and cannot be concerned with guards, angels, or gardeners. Her mind is exclusively on one track. She must find Jesus *as he was!* So when she hears that comfortingly familiar, "Mary!" what else is she to believe? "Rabboni!" she greets him. He is back again in the old relation. To here and the other friends of Jesus he had been Rabbi or Rabboni, the Master Teacher, their personal mentor. She does not yet know that she and all those other followers will soon give up that title to call him Lord! She still is aimed in an old direction and does not yet acknowledge an awareness of the radical change which Jesus represents.

Jesus tells Mary not to cling to him. It is unnecessary for her to hold on to him as though to protect the relationship. The wealth of meaning which is shared between them cannot be lost. She has yet to learn this, but she will learn that his radical change vouchsafes for us the precious knowledge which we have of those close to us. The resurrection keeps us close when the strongest pair of arms could not.

Jesus tells Mary not to cling to him. It is useless for her to try to hold on to the status quo. The present slips away from us dragging immediate sensations into the realm of pleasant but increasingly vague memories. There is no stopping this flow of time. God's future is open before us with all the promise of tomorrow and the strongest pair of arms cannot stay the course of redemptive history.

Mary need not hold to Jesus for she knows a relationship which cannot be lost and moments which cannot be kept except as memories.

Jesus speaks to a larger audience than just the girl from Magdalana. If we are wise enough, let us gain the understanding which is here for us. Two lessons are apparent to me.

The living Jesus finds us. For all her searching she would never have found Jesus. She looked for the one she knew in places where he was last seen. Jesus had to find her if there was to be a meeting. The radical nature of the resurrection is not discoverable by man. The biblical story of the resurrection of the body is not the same as Greek philosophy's speculation about the immortality of the soul. Resurrection is the revealed message of grace. Immortality is the speculation of reason which, more often than not, begins optimistically but then leads to a desperate despair. The desperation which comes as part of the human package is the necessary ingredient which opens us up to grace. But your desperation or mine will only bring us to our limits, our finiteness, our dependency. That's not all bad by any means. It represents quite a trip for most people I know. Sam Keen emphasizes the need to admit that the self is not divine, omnipotent, nor all-knowing. Keen mentions a friend who handed in his resignation "as manager of the universe" and was surprised at the quickness with which it was accepted.

Standing before death, that great leveler of humanity, that awesome definition of our limits, God's grace invades the scene to point to the resurrection of Jesus as a promise that the living Jesus will come in grace to our graves, too.

The second lesson from Mary's encounter with the resur-

Searching for Death, Finding Life

rected Jesus is *the living Jesus leans into the future.* Although the Bible is thoroughly historical literature, it has a decided forward cast to it. God's revelation consistently has a future-oriented lean. Carl Braaten observes that orthodoxy usually is caricatured as backward-looking and at a distance from those elements which because of their revolutionary tendencies have an eye for the future. But at least the first generation of Christians were fired by what they hoped was to come.

Augustine has characterized our stance toward time as requiring memory, consideration, and expectation. With these we view the past, the present, the future. The radical nature of the resurrection creates within us the ability to be expectant about the future. This expectancy means many things to the Christian.

The expectancy which is ours through the radical message of resurrection gives freedom. Expectancy enables Mary to let go of Jesus. An expectant attitude frees you to step into the future and away from the past.

This expectancy brings with it a boldness. Consider the witness of this woman. The radical experience with her resurrected Lord liberated her and her sisters beyond the understanding of Luther ("and she even a woman") fifteen hundred years later and chauvinists yet unborn.

Resurrection expectancy gives us hope. Perhaps hope is but another word for expectancy. It is a great word which Christians are rediscovering. Immanuel Kant has been frequently quoted as proposing three significant questions. "What can I know? What ought I to do? What may I hope?" wrote Kant in his *Critique of Pure Reason.* If we applied these to the American religious scene, they could approximate the interest of American churches for the more recent decades. "What can we know?" asked Christians at the turn of the century when doctrine was the concern and the liberal-fundamentalist controversy was the issue. "What ought we to do?" became the question as American churches turned toward ethics and faced up to social responsibility. Now with German theologians Pannenberg and Moltmann writing on the theology of hope and with an assist from catastrophic world politics we ask, "What may we hope?"

We are frantically helpless before world events, uncomfortable because of an energy crisis, suspicious because of an authority crisis, uncertain financially due to inflation and threatened recession—what may we hope? Is our search likely to be any more productive than Mary's thrashings? No, but thank God Mary's search did not reveal Christ; his grace did. And here is the grace of hope or the hope of grace, God surprises us with the radical future of the resurrection. There is an open-endedness about God's future. No one has the final word on what God might do next. In Braaten's words, "The element of contradiction is essential in the language of hope. Hope contradicts experience; the future will contradict the present—so we hope." And he goes on to quote Moltmann that our hope rests upon contradiction: "the contradiction of the resurrection to the cross."

As though we were sleepyheaded children before a Christmas tree not willing to believe our eyes, God contradicts our statement of life and death with his statement of radical resurrection grace.

The Gift of Clear Thought

The disciple whom Jesus loved said to Peter, "It is the Lord!" John 21:7

An article about a cryptologist awoke a spirit of nostalgia within me recently. The article said that this man was nudged into his profession because of an interest created when he read one of Edgar Allen Poe's stories. The story was about a man who struck out on a search while he was in the process of breaking a code. I was interested in the article because I had had the same response to Poe's story. I did not go into cryptology but I have had a lifelong interest in codes.

Perhaps I can create a similar interest in Bible study by reference to one of the biblical mysteries or problems that scholars consider: Who was the beloved disciple? Now literary research, or even Bible study, can sound very dry and boring to you. But it can be quite interesting and exciting. Perhaps if I could whet your appetite in this way for mystery research, we might have the serendipitous experience of finding information of deeper value than simply the identity of the beloved disciple.

If you should pursue that question, you would learn that the popular answer, and possibly the correct one is that the beloved disciple is John the son of Zebedee. But I will leave that puzzle for you to grapple with on your own. Find a good commentary and read the various arguments. Then make your own decision. Right now let's just see what the Fourth Gospel tells us about this mysterious disciple.

The beloved disciple is usually compared or contrasted with Peter in some way. At the Lord's Supper the beloved disciple is the intermediary between Peter and Jesus in asking about the betrayer. The mysterious disciple is one who is known at the high priest's house and is able to get Peter into the courtyard. He runs with Peter, in fact, outruns him to the empty tomb; and he is the first to believe the resurrection. While fishing one night, he is the first to recognize his Lord on the shore; Peter is the first to act upon that recognition. Finally, he is contrasted with Peter in the assignments they receive from their Lord.

There is one other possible notice of this mysterious follower in juxtaposition with Peter. In the first chapter, two of John the Baptist's disciples follow Jesus. One is Andrew who goes after Peter. The other is unnamed and may have been the beloved disciple (or James who goes to get his brother John). In a rough sense this could be the beginning of a novel account of "Peter and myself following Jesus." There is one further story about the beloved disciple which does not include Peter. That is the account of Jesus reciting to him and Mary a rough adoption formula from the cross.

Well, there is much to talk about and a good deal to speculate upon in recounting the appearances of the beloved disciple. The one message which I see, especially in the story of their various assignments, is the importance of accepting a suitable role in life.

The beloved disciple had certain gifts and responsibilities which were his alone. This is the point of chapter 21, and it is a lesson anyone can learn. The beloved disciple possessed the gift of insight. He had the responsibility of testimony.

Because of his gift of insight he was trusted. He had an

The Gift of Clear Thought

ability to understand quickly and at a deep level. He was trusted by Jesus and by Peter. Notice the difference between a dependable doer and a dependable thinker. This is not to say that the beloved disciple was undependable in action, but the emphasis is that they trusted his judgment.

He was trusted by Jesus. This is seen by his position as the Lord's Supper. He was to the right of Jesus. This was not the position of highest honor. Maybe Judas had that position? But to be on the right meant that he was a trusted friend. The scene at the cross shows that Jesus trusted him. Naturally, Jesus must have trusted him if he was willing to leave his mother in the beloved disciple's hands. And the overtones of chapter 21 along with the other stories strongly imply that there was understanding between the two of them at a deep level.

He was trusted by Peter. They were brought close through Jesus. They complemented one another. The two of them were quite similar and yet quite different. One was always the first to know. The other was always the first to do. And Peter quite often acted quickly on the basis of his friend's judgment.

It is interesting that the beloved disciple had sound judgment but he was not the leader. Jesus was the leader or Peter was. This disciple supported the leader with his understanding. How vital it is that some people say, "I have something very important to contribute, but someone else must be the head and I will support him with all my ability."

Because of his understanding he had the responsibility of communicating his insights. He was a witness to what had transpired in the life of Jesus. But he saw more than the events; he saw the meaning. He was charged to communicate the meaning. In a sense the beloved disciple was serving as a cryptologist. The events of life are nothing more than a puzzle to some people. Quite a few people saw what happened when Jesus came by, but not all had the ability to tell the story and include the meaning.

The title this man wears is an evidence of his role of communicating. The designation "beloved disciple" evidently comes out of the character of the man. Either he gave himself this title rather than use his name or a group of his followers gave it to him. Either way it says something about the force of the love of Jesus in his life. Notice he is not described as one who gives love but, more modestly, he is just the recipient of love. Even in this small way he is saying, or it is said about him, the point of my story is that Jesus loves. Isn't the best-known verse from his Gospel, "God so loved the world that he gave his only Son."

Love always shines through. It is told that once a young artist brought a picture of Jesus, which he had painted, to a well-known painter for his verdict upon it. But the verdict was slow in coming. When at last the opinion was given, it was in one sentence. "You don't love him, or you would paint him better."

Love always shines through. But the amazing thing is that we do not talk about how much the disciple loved Jesus; rather we call him the beloved disciple, meaning that the love of Jesus is so overpowering as to be seen in those he loves.

Well, that is a brief description of the beloved disciple. What does it mean to us?

First, there is the lesson of teamwork—the horizontal lesson. Teamwork within the Christian fellowship means that we exhibit trustworthiness. It means saying to one another, "I know there is much to be done in the life of our fellowship. You can depend on me to do what I am equipped by God to do."

Such teamwork also means for us to learn to trust the abilities of others rather than to covet them. "What about this other one, Lord? Will he have an assignment like mine?" "That is not really your concern, Peter." Rather than covet the ease, the glamor, or the notoriety that falls to another,

The Gift of Clear Thought

why not learn to depend upon the talents of your fellow in Christ?

In particular I want to challenge you to make use of the contributions of others which are available to you. If the other has the gift of listening and you need to talk, do so. If the other has the gift of insight and you need to learn, do so. You know you have a great deal of talent available to you in your church. And you may be wasting opportunities by not developing a dependent relationship within your Christian fellowship. I'm not talking about something neurotic. I am talking about a realistic relationship like that of the beloved disciple and Peter.

Second, there is the lesson of discipleship—the vertical lesson. Whatever responsibility we may have to our fellowmen, our responsibility is preeminently to God. Whatever gift may be yours, it is of God's grace and you are responsible to him who creates and sustains your life.

So what must you do? Accept yourself as you are. Discover what it is that you have that is so special. And be assured there is something special about you. Discover the purpose of your being and the need of your environment and put them together. Enhance your gift through development and use.

Discipline is what I am talking about. It means making the best of you—becoming the best that you can be, the you that God intends for you to be.

A Christian businessman named Marion Wade comments that people seem amused that he has dedicated his talents of "rug cleaning" and "killing moths" to God. Wade has written, "If the Lord himself was willing to dignify hard labor by working as a carpenter, any one of us can bring dignity to his job, whatever it is, by dedicating his efforts to God's glory."

To emphasize the truth that anyone's talents are useful in God's service, Wade tells the story of a hod carrier named Pat whose brother was a bishop. One day a friend remarked to

Pat, "The talents in your family are certainly unevenly divided." Pat's reply was, "Yes, my brother couldn't do my job to save his life!"

Whatever your talents may be, use them as a teammember and a disciple.

Disciplining Love

Lord, you know everything; you know that I love you! John 21:17 (RSV)

Where do nicknames originate? It is easy to see how one gets "Mac" from McDonald. And "Tex" needs no explanation. But some nicknames do call for a story.

For instance, my mother has been known as "Bun" since childhood. People often assume that "Bun" is some contraction of her name, Berniece. Actually the name stems from a pet rabbit. The pet is long forgotten but the name remains.

But why "Cephas"? In the first chapter of the Fourth Gospel there is the story of Andrew bringing his brother Simon to meet the Messiah. When Jesus sees this strapping fisherman he is prompted to give him a nickname. "Cephas" is the Hebrew form of the name, "Peter" is the Greek; in our idiom Simon gains the nickname "Rocky." Why? What is it that Jesus sees in Simon actually or potentially that calls for this name?

Simon Peter is a doer. He is a man with a strong sense of action. He is not one to sit still. Throughout the Fourth Gospel he is seen in motion: swinging a sword, running, swimming. The question is worth asking: Is there some characteristic of this motion-filled life that might have suggested a rock-

121

like personality?

Simon Peter is *bluntly inquisitive.* Jesus attempts to prepare his disciples for the disastrous events which will culminate in his death. In an attempt to soften the blow of his announcement he uses subtle terminology and speaks of leaving them. Peter is a literal, plainspoken soul and demands of Jesus, "Where ya goin'?"

Later Jesus announces that one of the group is a traitor. Immediately the disciples fall into introspection. "Is it I?" is the gasp of those about the table—except for Simon Peter. Simon Peter isn't given to turned-inward thoughts. He wears his heart and his mind on his sleeve. The others can sit around and guess to themselves all they want to; Simon Peter is not built that way. He motions to John, "Ask him who . . . ?"

In the Fourth Gospel with its mystical interpretations, double meanings, and subtle shadings, Simon Peter seems strangely out of place. He is plain spoken and bluntly inquisitive almost to the point of being rude. There is nothing subtle about a rock and, in that sense, perhaps the name fits.

Simon Peter is *both impatient and obstinant.* Before the final passover meal with his disciples, Jesus begins to wash their dusty feet. But Simon Peter will have none of it. The master tries to explain something about his actions to the effect that "now" may be a puzzle but "then" the disciples will understand. Cephas—"Rocky"—has no room for "then" in his vocabulary. He wants answers to his bluntly put questions *now!*

When Jesus attempts to wash Peter's feet, the fisherman firmly denies him the chance. "You will never wash my feet, never!" Quickly Jesus breaks down this obstinancy by showing how important it is for Simon Peter to allow him to perform this menial task. Then the big palooka goes to the other extreme and wants a complete bath.

It seems contradictory to say that he is both impatient and obstinant. Again, however, these attributes are his and could

Discipling Love

be the cause of his nickname "Rocky." When a rock starts rolling it is hard to stop; it will not be denied. On the other hand, when a rock has found its place, it becomes almost immovable.

Simon Peter is definitely a man who is *impulsive and overly confident.* His impulsiveness is a combination of his plainly literal style of thought and the impatience of his spirit. He protests to his leader, "I am ready to die for you!" When suddenly they are surprised in the garden by a band of Temple guards, Simon Peter foolishly lashes out with a sword. His action is rash. He acts on the impulse of the moment with no uncertainties, no doubts about himself.

If it had not been for the quick action of Jesus, the whole little covey of disciples might have been obliterated, all due to the fisherman's bold but foolish gesture. Simon Peter's impulsive overconfidence stems from a lack of awareness or appreciation for his weaknesses.

Perhaps somewhere in these personality traits is an explanation of the nickname "Rocky." And yet, they do not add up to anything rock-like. Arthur John Gossip identifies the outstanding feature of Simon as "a queer undependability." Who could miss seeing an impetuousness about the man that makes him an unstable variable in the Gospel accounts?

I believe there is something else about Simon Peter, however, that had its first glimmer when he and Jesus met through Andrew's introduction. This attribute can be seen growing in almost every scene where Simon Peter is shown in the Fourth Gospel. Simon Peter shows *a deeply felt, free-flowing love for Jesus.* This attribute, which showed itself seminally on a first meeting, has a potential for being the foundation of a useful life.

"Rocky's" free-flowing love shows up consistently. Here Jesus is discouraged by the crowds that turn away. He asks his closest friends, "Will you also go?" Out of love for his discouraged leader Peter quickly replies, "To whom would we go?"

Can't you see the love behind the refusal to let Jesus wash his feet and the quick capitulation that asks a thorough cleansing?

Love prompts the request to John to ask the name of the betrayer. Love underlies the argument, "Why can't we go with you. I am ready to do anything—to even die—with you!"

Love motivated the foolish attack upon Malchus. As with all of these events, love pushed Simon Peter as he ran to the tomb, swam to the shore, rushed to the side of his master.

The beloved disciple was chosen to bear the responsibility of caring for Jesus' mother—a notable sign of close relationship. But I am convinced that of all the disciples, Simon Peter was the one who was the closest friend of Jesus.

Love is a fuel. It propels one. But just as an engineer designs more than a fuel system into a rocket, a life needs something besides propulsion. There must also be a guidance system, a sense of direction.

Simon Peter begins to have difficulties when his strong feelings are combined with some of those attributes which make him impulsive. His "queer undependability" brings him to boasting about future attitudes and actions which he cannot fulfill. Surely he wanted to show his love through actions. Certainly he thought he could do as he promised. But he misjudges his own weaknesses and, in the end, he denies his best friend.

The author skillfully joins the story of Peter denying Jesus in the courtyard with the story of Jesus affirming his identity and his mission in the presence of Annas. Even though this disciple is but a few scant yards away, Jesus has been abandoned by him. The great tragedy is that this denial was totally opposed to the genuine love that Simon Peter felt for Jesus.

I said that "in the end" "Rocky" denied his best friend. Fortunately that isn't true. Deny his friend he did, but that

Discipling Love

was not the end. Peter was impulsive but not like Judas. "Rocky" did not take his life in despair. He runs, swims, rushes to Jesus and reconciliation. There with his Lord is the thrice repeated cycle:

"Do you love me?"

"Yes! and you know it to be true. And," Peter implies, "I know that you know it."

"Tend my flocks."

Jesus gives his good friend a chance to voice his love before their comrades. He allows Simon Peter to realize that Jesus accepts his love and honors that love with his assignment. And what an assignment! The Old Testament image of the shepherd is strong. He is an authoritative figure as well as a compassionate one. That image was a major theme for Jesus in describing his own role. And so, Jesus is saying to his good friend: "I know you love me. I accept that love. And I commission your use of that love in my service."

That assignment is strong but there is ballast to the authority given. The job is Simon Peter's but the sheep are the Lord's. Peter has been overly confident. His impatient spirit was ready to act at any given moment. He operated under the delusion that he was self-sufficient. Through painful experience and a patient teacher he was learning that accomplishment requires divine commission as much as human response.

The combination of experience and teaching must have taken effect because Jesus tells his close friend that his service of love will lead finally to the surrender of his life. For the first time Jesus acknowledges as a possibility what Simon Peter had boasted of continually: Jesus finally agrees that it might be possible for Simon Peter to give his life for his Master. Of course improvement does not mean complete change. "Rocky" immediately points out the beloved disciple asking, "What about him?" And the rebuke is not so harsh as some would think. "Oh, come on now Rocky! You know that is none of your business!"

Two simple points can be gleaned from this life. The first is: *Love needs controls.* You cannot simply give love its head (Or should I say its heart?). "Love God and do as you please," sounds quite exalted, but it is incomplete as a guide for the Christian life. Love can motivate. It is a fuel and can propel a life. But love does not of itself define what is the best course of action. Without wisdom, love is impulsive, impetuous, and sometimes dangerous.

Quite often Simon Peter functions under the control of the insights of John. They make a good combination for a time. The intent of Jesus seems to be to get "Rocky" to take some of the responsibility for thinking first upon his own shoulders.

The second point I would like to make is: *Love needs expression.* Stewardship calls for the use of love's force. Yes, John's insight often guides Peter's action; but there are occasions where John is brought to action because of Peter's boldness. Jesus speaks of betrayal and the story seems to catch up and the drama moves forward again. John runs to the empty tomb but his body seems frozen there as his mind races about in frantic circles. The draft from "Rocky's" boldness pulls the hesitant beloved disciple into the tomb where the impact of the resurrection can break upon his mind.

The first chapter of Peter's second epistle describes a pyramid of eight virtues which culminate in love. It may indicate how well "Rocky" learned his lessons to note that two of the virtues listed are knowledge and self-control.

Would that we all could learn as well!